WHY

DOES THE
EARTH
NEED THE
MOON?

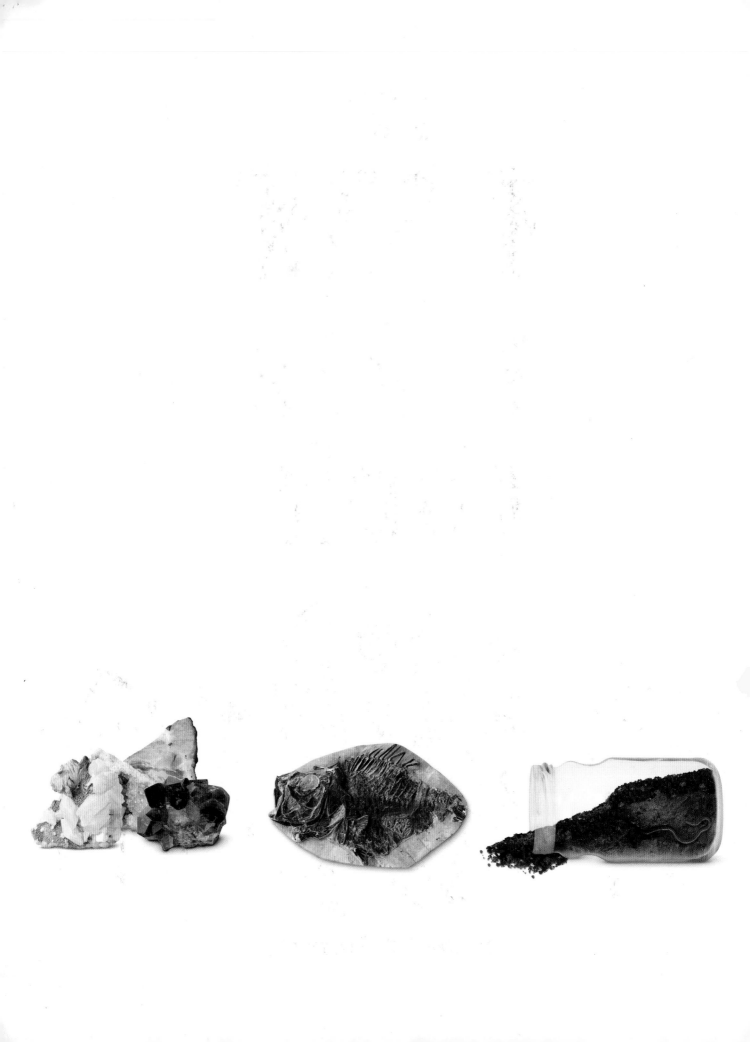

WHY

DOES THE
EARTH
NEED THE
MOON?

Dr. Devin Dennie

DK | Penguin Random House

Author Dr Devin Dennie
Consultants Jonathan Dale, Prof. David M. Schultz, Prof. Richard Worden
Illustrator Dan Crisp

DK LONDON
Editor Kathleen Teece
Senior designer Fiona Macdonald
Additional editing Olivia Stanford, Katie Lawrence
Managing editor Laura Gilbert
Managing art editor Diane Peyton Jones
Pre-production producer Nikoleta Parasaki
Producer Isabell Schart
Jacket designer Steven Marsden
Jacket editor Francesca Young
Creative director Helen Senior
Publishing director Sarah Larter

DK DELHI
Editors Anwesha Dutta, Shambhavi Thatte
Designers Kartik Gera, Shipra Jain, Jaileen Kaur, Nidhi Mehra, Nehal Verma, Mohd Zishan
Managing editor Alka Thakur Hazarika
Managing art editor Romi Chakraborty
DTP designers Mohammad Rizwan, Dheeraj Singh
CTS manager Balwant Singh
Production manager Pankaj Sharma
Picture researcher Aditya Katyal
Delhi team head Malavika Talukder

First published in Great Britain in 2019 by
Dorling Kindersley Limited
80 Strand, London, WC2R 0RL

A CIP catalogue record for this book
is available from the British Library.
ISBN: 978-0-2413-5837-5

Printed and bound in China

A WORLD OF IDEAS:
SEE ALL THERE IS TO KNOW

www.dk.com

Contents

Our planet

The Earth's surface

Blue planet

Up in the air

Living on the Earth

Find out why I became extinct on page 112.

Discover which tiny creatures are hidden in moss on page 60.

Our planet

We are floating in space on a rocky planet called the Earth. It is part of an eight-planet Solar System that circles the Sun (a star). The Earth is just at the right distance from the Sun for life to exist, which makes our planet unique.

Space debris

Rocks, gas, and lumps of dirty ice once filled the space where the Earth would form. Around 4.5 billion years ago, a force called gravity began to pull the pieces together to form a mini planet called a planetoid.

The growing Earth

Over millions of years, the Earth grew as more debris smashed into it. The explosive impacts caused the Earth's surface to melt. Heavy metals sank to the centre to form the Earth's core.

How did the Earth form?

The Earth was once space dust. The Sun came into existence about 4.6 billion years ago. It pulled gas, ice, and rocks into circles around it called orbits. This spinning rubble collided to form the planets in our Solar System, including the Earth.

Is the Earth round?

The Earth is round but not a true sphere. It is slightly egg shaped! This is because the Earth rotates. The strong force of the rotation makes it bulge out in the middle.

The Earth today

Rocks continue to melt in the Earth's hot centre and re-form its surface. Modern-day continents look very different from earlier land masses.

Cooling down

By 4 billion years ago, most objects in the Earth's path had already hit the planet. The pressure from the Earth's outer layers kept the core hot. Surface rocks cooled to form a solid crust.

Oceans form

Water escaped from surface rocks about 3.8 billion years ago to form oceans. Light rocks of the crust rose to the top as continents.

Sun

How hot is the Sun?

The corona is the outermost layer of the Sun's atmosphere. It can reach around 1.7 million °C (3.1 million °F). The inner core is even hotter. Here, temperatures can soar to 16 million °C (28.8 million °F).

space begins at the Karman line, 100 km (62 miles) above the Earth.

How does the atmosphere keep us safe?

The Earth's layered atmosphere is like a protective blanket. It keeps us warm, gives us gas to breathe, and blocks the Sun's harmful radiation. The Earth would be hit by more space rocks if they didn't burn up as they fell through the atmosphere.

Exosphere

This zone is just before outer space. Satellites and the International Space Station are found here. It starts at around 500 km (310 miles) above the Earth.

Thermosphere

Here, temperatures can get very high because gas particles absorb lots of the Sun's energy.

Karman line

Mesosphere

Meteors get hot and burn up by rubbing against the many gas particles in this layer.

See pages 132–133 for the answer

? Picture quiz

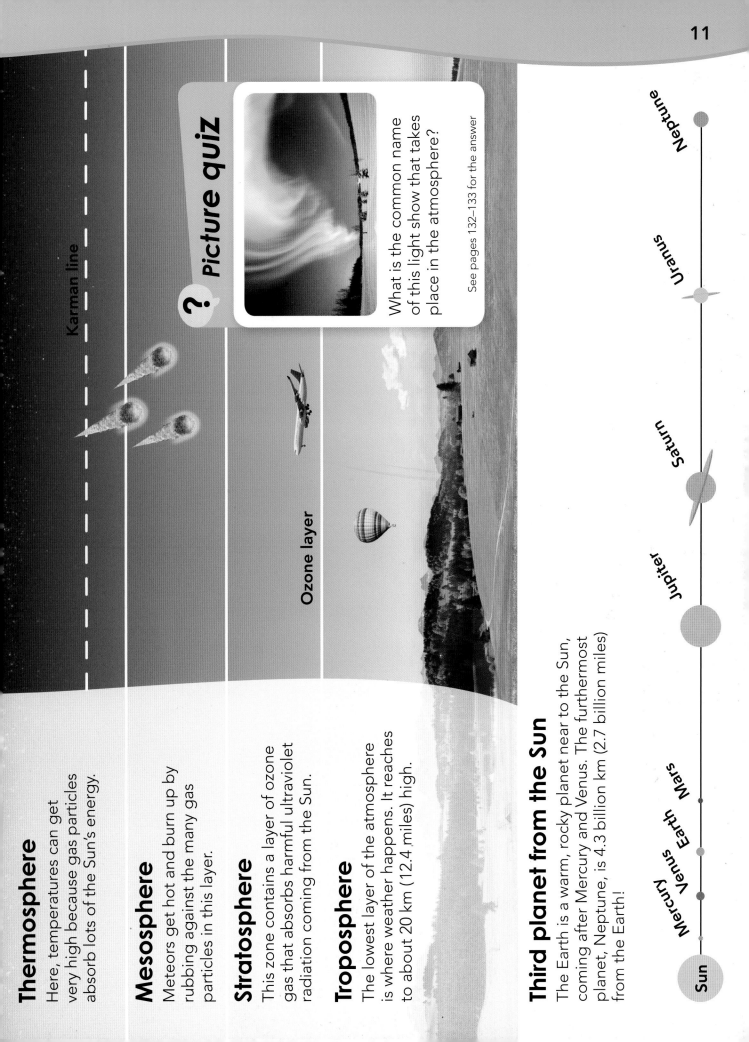

What is the common name of this light show that takes place in the atmosphere?

Stratosphere

This zone contains a layer of ozone gas that absorbs harmful ultraviolet radiation coming from the Sun.

Ozone layer

Troposphere

The lowest layer of the atmosphere is where weather happens. It reaches to about 20 km (12.4 miles) high.

Third planet from the Sun

The Earth is a warm, rocky planet near to the Sun, coming after Mercury and Venus. The furthermost planet, Neptune, is 4.3 billion km (2.7 billion miles) from the Earth!

Sun

Mercury

Venus

Earth

Mars

Jupiter

Saturn

Uranus

Neptune

Hidden Sun

The Sun still shines at night – but on the other side of the Earth! Our planet blocks out the light.

The Earth's axis

The Earth spins around an imaginary line called an axis. This runs between the two poles.

North Pole

South Pole

Rotation

The Earth spins on its axis

The Earth

The Earth rotates in space, spinning like a top as it revolves around the Sun.

Where does the Sun go at night?

The Sun doesn't go anywhere! The reason you can't see it at night is because the Earth spins. As the day passes, your country is turned to face the opposite direction to the Sun.

? Quick quiz

1. What is a meteorite?

2. Does the Sun move around the Earth?

See pages 132–133 for the answers

Visible Sun

You can see the Sun when your side of the Earth is facing it. Sometimes, the Moon moves to block the Sun in an eclipse.

The Sun

The Sun is our nearest star. It is huge and very hot inside. It gives out light and heat.

Light from the Sun

Light from the Sun travels through space to the Earth. This gives us daylight.

What are shooting stars?

Meteor

These are bodies of rock or ice in space. They were left over from the formation of the Solar System, 4.5 billion years ago. Some "shooting stars" are no bigger than a grain of sand!

Meteorite

When a larger meteor falls to the Earth in one piece, the rock we find is called a meteorite.

How is the Earth like an onion?

Both the Earth and onions have layers! Heavy rocks and metals sink down inside the Earth and lighter material rises. This creates layers of metal and rock. Heat and pressure deeper within cause some layers to melt.

Crust

The solid outer layer is made up of cold rocks. It is brittle and can break like toffee. The aesthenosphere and crust form the lithosphere.

Upper mantle

This warm layer has lower pressure than the layers beneath. Its upper portions flow slowly, like toothpaste.

Lower mantle

This rigid layer of hot rock is under so much pressure from outer layers that it can't melt or flow.

Outer core

This metallic zone is so hot that it melts into liquid. The metal spins around the Earth's inner core.

Inner core

This is an ultra-hot, solid ball of iron and nickel metal. Huge pressure stops it from melting.

Aesthenosphere

This gooey layer is just beneath the crust. It is hot, with low pressure, causing rocks to melt into magma.

Types of crust

The crust is made up of two types. Oceanic crust beneath oceans is thin and dense. Continental crust is thicker and less dense. It is lighter than oceanic crust.

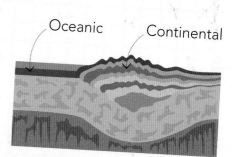

Oceanic   Continental

How far down have humans dug?

The Kola Superdeep Borehole in Kola Peninsula, Russia, is the deepest well ever drilled. It is 12 km (7.5 miles) deep. This is over 15 times the height of the Burj Khalifa in Dubai, the tallest building in the world!

Kola Superdeep Borehole

15 Burj Khalifas

? Quick quiz

1. Is the inner core of the Earth solid?

2. What is the name of the layer of magma beneath the Earth's crust?

3. Is the Earth's crust all in one piece?

See pages 132–133 for the answers

Onion

Onions grow layer by layer. Like the Earth, these layers get thinner as they get closer to the surface.

Why don't things float off the Earth?

A force called gravity sticks us to the Earth. This force pulls things together. The Sun's gravity keeps the Earth nearby. Without the Earth's gravity, we'd all float away!

Weaker pull
All objects pull things towards them using gravity, but the pull is much weaker for small objects.

Is there gravity everywhere in space?

The Earth's neighbourhood
The Earth's gravity pulls spacecraft around it. They fall through space, and astronauts fall too, so they appear to float!

Outer space
Even in the furthest reaches of space there is gravity. The gravity of far-off stars spreads out around them for massive distances.

? *True or false?*

1. The Sun pulls the Earth towards it with gravity.

2. Dogs have a tiny force of gravity.

3. There is no gravity in outer space.

See pages 132–133 for the answers

Orbital gravity

Gravity from large objects in space pulls other objects into circular paths called orbits. They keep moving but can't escape the pull.

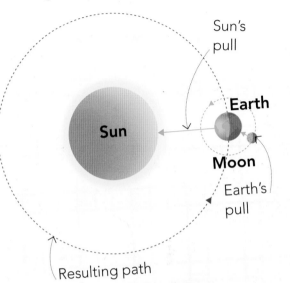

Sun's pull

Earth

Sun

Moon

Earth's pull

Resulting path

GRAY-NICOLLS

The Earth's gravity

Gravity is stronger the nearer an object is. When you stand right on the Earth's surface, you experience maximum gravity.

Why can't we live on Mars?

Humans need liquid water and air with lots of oxygen to survive. The only planet these are found on is the Earth. Some scientists are planning a human-made colony on Mars, but we couldn't live outside on the freezing, low-oxygen surface.

Goldilocks zone

The Earth is not too hot and not too cold, like the porridge in *Goldilocks and the Three Bears*. Water here doesn't all freeze or turn to steam, so plants can grow. These make oxygen for us to breathe.

Too hot

As the closest planets to the Sun, Mercury and Venus are just too hot. Gases in Venus's atmosphere trap the heat to make it even hotter. The lack of gas on Mercury makes it freezing at night.

Venus

Mercury

Sun

The Sun makes energy that hits planets as light and creates heat. Each planet gets a different amount of energy.

Too cold

Mars is too cold because of its distance from the Sun. The only water here is frozen at the poles or underground.

Mars

Earth

Are there other habitable planets?

There are billions of planets in the Universe. We have recently found ones that may be similar to the Earth, such as Kepler-62f.

? Picture quiz

Which planet comes after Mars?

See pages 132–133 for the answer

Did the chicken or egg come first?

The first ever chicken hatched out of an egg from an earlier species! Life on the Earth faces many challenges. Over time, babies with features that help them to better survive are born and flourish. This process is called evolution.

Chickens eat stones to help them grind down food in their gizzards. Dinosaurs had gizzards too!

Dinosaur egg

Dinosaurs hatched out of eggs just like birds do. This is because birds evolved from dinosaurs.

Fluffy feathers

Velociraptors had feathers and were not much bigger than chickens. Both species evolved from the same unknown dinosaur.

How do we know about evolution?

DNA
What we look like depends on our DNA. Similar DNA shows that species are related.

Fossil
Fossils are remains of ancient creatures. The features of some fossils can be found in animals today.

Peppered moth
Dark peppered moths became more common than light coloured moths because they could hide from predators.

? Quick quiz

1. How old are the remains of the oldest bacteria?

2. Are crocodiles related to dinosaurs?

3. When did dinosaurs become extinct?

See pages 132–133 for the answers

First life on the Earth

Blob-like amoebas and bacteria were the first living things. The oldest bacteria was found in rocks that are 4 billion years old!

Amoeba

Dinosaur descendants

A huge extinction event wiped out most of the dinosaurs 65 million years ago. Some small descendants survived and evolved into birds.

Terrifying talons

Birds such as chickens have many dinosaur-like features. They have hollow, light skeletons, similar lungs and hearts, and talons!

Does land stay still?

The Earth's surface is always moving, but usually so slowly that we can't feel it. In the past, this motion caused the continents to collide, forming a supercontinent. The continents may collide again, many millions of years in the future.

Changing continents

Northern Pangaea became North America, Europe, and parts of Asia. Southern Pangaea broke up into South America, Africa, Australia, Antarctica, and India.

The seven continents today

Supercontinent

Creatures living on the Earth around 330 to 175 million years ago could walk from America to Africa across one joined-up continent called Pangaea.

Eurasia

North America

Jigsaw continents

Modern South America looks like it would fit right into West Africa if you pushed the two continents together like a jigsaw. This is evidence they were once joined.

South America

Africa

Australasia

Antarctica

One ocean

When Pangaea existed, one ocean covered most of the rest of the Earth. Called Panthalassa, this became the Pacific, Atlantic, and Indian oceans we know today.

What clues suggest that the continents were once joined together?

Plant fossils

Plants can't spread their seeds across oceans, so similar fossils found across continents suggest a connected land.

Dinosaur fossils

Similar dinosaur remains found on different continents suggest they could once walk from one continent to the other.

? Picture quiz

The remains of which African animal have been found in Derbyshire, UK?

See pages 132–133 for the answer

Did everywhere freeze in the last ice age?

An ice age occurs when the Earth gets colder and ice covers large parts of it. The last ice age was from around 108,000 BCE to 10,000 BCE. Many of today's cities would have been under ice, but the warm equator stayed mostly ice-free.

Last ice age

Over the 100,000 years tha made up the last ice age, huge ice sheets, or glaciers covered many places where there are now cities.

North America

The locations of New York and other northern US cities were once under ice up to 1.6 km (1 mile) thick.

South America

What is now Caracas in Venezuela and most of the rest of South America were too warm for ice to form.

Can woolly mammoths come back to life?

A chemical in animals' bodies called DNA contains instructions on how the animal first formed. The DNA of a mammoth frozen in ice is being studied to possibly re-create this huge animal.

The Arctic

The Arctic was a thick and massive ice sheet in the last ice age. Today, many parts are still locked in ice.

? Quick quiz

1. How thick did ice sheets get during the last ice age?

2. When did the last ice age end?

3. Was the location of New York City once under ice?

See pages 132–133 for the answers

Europe

The locations of Warsaw and other northern European cities were under ice. Southern city sites were cool but without ice.

Africa

What is now Nouakchott in Mauritania and many other parts of Africa are near the equator. Places such as this would have been ice-free.

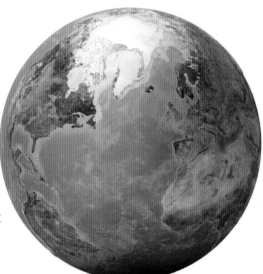

Interglacial

The periods of melting between ice ages are called interglacials. Today, we are in an interglacial period. It is warmer and most of the glaciers from the last ice age have melted.

The Earth's surface

The Earth's surface is always changing. Water, wind, and ice wear down its rocks and soil to create new and wonderful landforms. Heat deep inside the Earth melts rock, turning it into lava that erupts from volcanoes and magma from which whole continents form.

Do mountains grow?

Mountains get bigger, but you'd have to watch one for a long time to see it grow! Underground, the Earth is divided into moving rocky segments, or plates. These collide, or bump into each other, and push each other up into mountain ranges, such as the Himalayas.

Young mountains

The Himalayas are relatively young mountains. Some mountain ranges are over a billion years old.

How did the Himalayas form?

The Himalayas formed around 40 to 50 million years ago, when the continental plate beneath India crashed into the Eurasian plate.

The plates collide

The mountains are pushed up further

Collision

When India crashed into the southern edge of Eurasia, the rock was forced up and out of the ground.

Growing mountains

The plates are still slowly pushing against each other today, so the mountains continue to rise.

ising peaks

he Himalayan peaks rise by
bout 5 mm (0.2 in) every year.

all of mountains

oung mountain ranges
re like solid walls of rock
ecause water and wind
aven't worn them
own very much.

? True or false?

1. Mauna Kea was formed
   by plates colliding.

2. Mountains grow over time.

3. The Himalayas are the
   oldest mountain range
   in the world.

See pages 132–133 for the answers

How else do mountains form?

Mountains can form from volcanoes.
Over time, molten rock called lava erupts
out of the volcano and hardens to form
igneous rock. This rock can build up into
high volcanic mountains, such as Mauna
Kea in Hawaii.

Are volcanic flows slow or fast?

You could outwalk or outrun most lava flows. However, not all eruptions are the same. Some lava streams can flow up to 64 kph (40 mph), while others may explode violently!

Lava

Magma that erupts above ground is called lava. Thick and very hot lava flows slowly. Coole lighter lava containing gas may explode into columns of ash.

Eruption

Molten rock called magma is found deep underground. It can rise up and erupt through fissures (cracks) in the ground. As each layer of lava cools, it can form a steep stratovolcano that gets bigger with more eruptions.

Volcanic ash

Magma rises

Fissures

Magma chamber

Stratovolcano

Are there different types of volcano?

Caldera

Calderas are large, cone-shaped depressions, often containing valleys or lakes. They are made when volcanoes collapse after the magma from underground chambers is released.

Cinder cone

These landforms are created when hot lava is shot out of the ground and hardens into cinders, or tiny bits of rock. The cinders build up to form a cone.

Shield

Shield volcanoes are made of stacks of hardened layers of lava. Mauna Loa, on the island of Hawaii, is a giant shield volcano.

Ash cloud

Burning material called ash erupts from volcanoes. Some super-hot, gassy ash clouds can erupt at 322 kph (200 mph)!

? True or false?

1. The temperature of some lava is over 1,500 °C (2,732 °F).

2. Lava is rock.

See pages 132–133 for the answers

What happens when water gets superheated?

Some water is found underground in chambers. Here, the water can get warmed to high temperatures by heat coming from deep inside the Earth. The hot water can find its way to the surface, causing a variety of unique landforms.

Steam

Superheated water deep underground boils and flashes to steam. This provides the energy for the geyser to erupt.

Porous rock

Surface water can move down through holes and cracks in the rock. The water heats up as it trickles down.

What are the other features of natural hot water?

Hot springs

Hot springs are features where hot water emerges from the ground. It is warmed underground by hot rocks.

Mudpots

When hot springs happen in areas with volcanic ash or mud, they mix to form a thick, gloopy sludge. These are called mudpots.

Geyser

Underground water rises quickly, flashing into steam. The steam billows out, pushing water to the surface at over 80 kph (50 mph)!

Underground heat

Rocks deep within the Earth are heated by the Earth's super-hot core. Water present in the rocks helps the rocks melt.

Quick quiz

1. What mixes into hot springs to form mudpots?

2. Where is the Earth's tallest geyser?

3. How high can water from the Steamboat Geyser reach?

See pages 132–133 for the answers

Steamboat Geyser in Yellowstone National Park, USA, is the Earth's tallest geyser!

The front part of this geyser has been cut away to show the hot water inside.

Is soil made of animals?

Soil is a mixture of different materials, including animal remains! The make-up of soil depends on the types of rocks and plants in an area, as well as the climate, slope, and how long it took to form.

Soil horizons

Soil can be divided into horizontal, or sideways, layers called horizons. These develop as surface materials are affected by air, water, and living things. Each layer was formed differently and has a unique soil type.

Animal remains

When animals die, their bodies break down into smaller bits inside soil. This process is called decomposition.

Minerals

Tiny bits of natural material called minerals break off rocks and become part of soil.

? True or false?

1. The leaching layer is the top layer of soil.

2. Peat can be burned for heat and fossil-fuel energy.

3. Rain can wash away loose soil.

See pages 132–133 for the answers

Sandy soil

Sand-sized soil grains can be up to 2 mm (0.08 in) big. There are holes between the grains that allow the soil to store plenty of air and water.

Humus

Top soil

Leaching layer

Subsoil

Bedrock

Horizon layers

Why are soils in danger?

Soil can be washed away by rain. Tree roots help to hold soil in place so that it isn't washed away. When trees are cut down for wood or to clear land, rain carries away the loose soil.

Earthworm

Worms help to disturb, digest, and turn over soil, which breaks down plants quicker.

Peaty soil

Some soils are rich in broken-down plant materials called peat, which is found in marshes or bogs.

Void space

Air and water are stored in soil. This soil moisture is important for plants and for gluing soil together.

Plants

Leaves and other dead bits of plant break down to become part of soil.

Do I contain minerals?

Minerals are natural solids, but they aren't alive. They are found everywhere, including in our food and in our bodies. There are many different kinds of minerals. Gemstones and some metal ores are minerals.

Calcium in teeth

Did you know that you had rocks inside your head? Your teeth contain the mineral hydroxyapatite, which is made up of calcium. Calcium in food and drink helps make teeth strong.

Serpentine

Celestine

Sulphur

Vegetables

When vegetables grow, the roots of their plants take in minerals and water from the soil. These minerals help the plant to grow bigger.

Crystal structure

Minerals grow in crystal shapes. The smallest part of an object is an atom. Atoms are lined up neatly to make the different crystal shapes.

Cubic crystal

Hexagonal crystal

Tetragonal crystal

Triclinic crystal

? True or false?

1. Ice is a mineral.

2. Teeth contain minerals.

3. Minerals are alive.

See pages 132–133 for the answers

Minerals

Gemstones and other minerals are made up of special crystal shapes. Different minerals have unique colours and textures.

Garnet

Rose quartz

Opal

Silicate mineral

Many minerals contain a natural material called silica. These are called silicates. A wide variety of minerals contain silica, including amethyst.

Amethyst

What are minerals used for?

Minerals have a variety of uses. Many types of toothpaste contain silica, which helps to rub your teeth clean. Medicines such as antacids, which help get rid of gas in your tummy, also contain minerals.

Which rock should I build with?

Rocks have been used for statues and as building blocks for thousands of years because of their hardness, toughness, and overall strength. Different types of rock have different levels of strength.

Which is the strongest mineral?

Rocks are made of minerals. The Mohs scale orders minerals by hardness, and diamond has the top ranking of 10! This makes it the hardest mineral. Diamonds are found underground or can be created by humans.

White marble

Marble is limestone that has been squashed deep underground. It is stronger than limestone because the minerals inside are more tightly packed.

Granite

Granite is one of the toughest stones on Earth. It's made up of hard minerals such as quartz and feldspar, making it strong.

Limestone and concrete

Limestone is made of a soft mineral called calcite. However, it is the basis for concrete, one of the world's most important building materials. Concrete is not easily worn down, unlike natural limestone. ••••••

Bust of a man, Cyprus

Sedimentary rock

This type of rock is often soft, and is worn away by weather more easily than other types of rock. It is made of squished sediment, such as sand, or the remains of ancient plants and animals.

Bust of Venus, Italy

Metamorphic rock

This type of rock has been through intense heat and pressure from being buried deep in the Earth or from extreme heating.

Colossal granite head of Amenhotep III, Egypt

Igneous rock

Igneous rocks such as granite cool and harden from molten rock underground. As they grow, the mineral crystals inside lock together to form very strong rocks.

? Quick quiz

1. The Mohs scale measures
   a) Wetness
   b) Hardness
   c) Size

2. A metamorphic rock is a rock that has undergone
   a) Heat and pressure
   b) Being worn away by the weather
   c) Being cut by humans

See pages 132–133 for the answers

Can a cliff turn into sand?

Cliffs might seem strong, but bits of rock are always breaking off. Water, wind, and ice break down rock into sand. This process is called weathering. Parts of this canyon in the Yellowstone National Park, USA, have been worn away over time.

Water in rock

In winter, water freezes in tiny holes and cracks inside rock. The hard ice expands, breaking the rock down into smaller pieces.

River

Flowing water picks up large rocks. The rocks break apart into smaller pieces as they roll and bounce along.

Wind

Strong winds can carry sand. The sand slowly scratches and sculpts rocks over time.

Are there beaches made of Grand Canyon rock?

The Colorado River carries sand from the Grand Canyon in Arizona, USA, to the Pacific Ocean. Currents and waves carry the sand onto beaches such as Big Sur, California, USA.

Sand

This sand was once part of larger rocks in the cliffs above. The rock was carried away and broken down by the river.

? Quick quiz

1. When did the Grand Canyon of the Yellowstone form?

2. What is the process that breaks down rock called?

3. Can humans wear rock down by walking on it?

See pages 132–133 for the answers

Why do rocks form amazing shapes?

Water, wind, and ice transform our landscapes in a process called erosion. They create interesting landforms like the Wave, which swishes through a valley in Arizona, USA.

Flowing water

These sandstone rocks record an ancient sea that broke off bits of rock as it flowed over them millions of years ago.

How does water erosion happen?

Water carries bits of rock called sediment away from one place and drops it off in another. By removing parts, the shape of the rock left behind is changed.

Water cuts through rock

Sediment is carried by water

What types of rocky landforms are there?

Natural bridge
These form when a stream or river erodes softer rock from below a stronger rock, leaving a natural bridge.

Canyon
As erosion carries away sediment, a hollow called a canyon forms. Over millions of years, this process created the Grand Canyon in the USA.

Tower
These upright rock formations are what remain after a lot of erosion. Similar shapes include spires, hoodoos, and fairy chimneys.

Ancient dunes
Vast areas of sand dunes occupied parts of the supercontinent that once contained the USA. The Wave is what's left of some of them.

Varied colours
The stripy colours in this rock came from minerals that were deposited as water flowed through holes in the stone.

? Quick quiz

1. What do the colours in the Wave show?

2. Which river wore away rocks to create the Grand Canyon, USA?

3. What type of rock is the Wave made of?

See pages 132–133 for the answers

Could I become a fossil?

Fossils are the rocky remains of plants and animals that lived long, long ago. The fossils most people think of are dinosaur bones, but many different kinds can be found. Even you could become a fossil one day, if you were buried deeply enough!

Coprolites are fossilized poo!

A fish dies and sinks to the ocean floor.

The bones are left when the rest of the body is eaten or decays.

The ocean begins to dry.

Sediment builds up

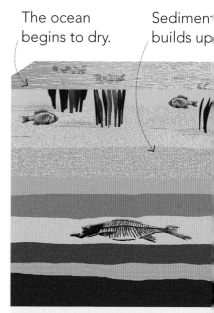

Death

Fossils start out as living things, such as fish. After death, soft parts of the body, such as skin and other organs, begin to be eaten away by worms or other fish.

Decay

The bones are left behind. They start to be covered by sediment, such as sand and mud. Over time, layers of sediment build up to cover the skeleton.

Rock forms

Sediment buries the skeleton deep underground. Fluids and the pressure of a the ground pressing down hardens the sediment and fish into new rock.

What are some other examples of fossils?

Moulds
When living things die and rot away, they can leave the outline of their shapes, such as shells, in the ground. These are called moulds.

Buried in amber
Amber is made of fossilized tree resin. Insects get caught in the sticky liquid, which hardens around them, preserving the body.

? *True or false?*

1. Sea creatures are most likely to become fossils.

2. Trace fossils start out as bones or shells.

3. The word "fossil" comes from *fodere*, the Latin word for dig.

See pages 132–133 for the answers

Fish and other marine animals are the most common fossils.

Scientists called palaeontologists dig up fossils using tools.

Discovery
Millions of years later, the ocean floor is raised up into a mountain range, or exposed when sea levels fall.

Body fossil
Different types of fossil have distinct shapes. Body fossils are bones or hard shells that have become rock. Trace fossils record movements of living things, such as footprints.

The rock around fossils gives clues about the time when the organism lived.

Can you freeze in a desert?

Deserts are known for being smoulderingly hot, but they also get so cold that a person might freeze! Deserts receive less than 25 cm (10 in) of rain each year. This means there isn't enough water in the air to hold heat once the Sun goes down.

Cold desert

The Gobi Desert in Asia is cold all year round! It's still a desert because it has barely any wet weather. A dusting of snow might be carried by wind from Siberia, though.

Antarctica is the largest desert in the world. It covers an area of 14 million sq km (5.5 million sq miles)!

High altitude

Alpine deserts form where air is cold and thin and there isn't much precipitation, or rain and snow. Very little vegetation grows this high up.

Can living things survive in cold deserts?

Bactrian camel

Camels are animals built for dry desert living. They can go for months without drinking water and store excess fat for energy in their two large humps.

Saltwort

This grass can consume the salty water common in many deserts. Animals don't eat the salty plant, and its low freezing point means it can survive in low temperatures.

? True or false?

1. The coldest place on Earth is at the top of Mount Everest.

2. Deserts are hot at night.

See pages 132–133 for the answers

How does a sinkhole sink?

Certain types of rock can dissolve, or wear down, below the Earth's surface. This causes a void, or empty space. The surface can eventually sink inward into the void to form a sinkhole.

Formation of a sinkhole

Acidic liquids can dissolve certain types of rock, such as limestone. Rainwater is slightly acidic and starts to dissolve some of the rock in the ground.

A cave forms as more and more rock is dissolved. The cave slowly enlarges. The roof of rock above gets thinner. This starts to form cracks.

The roof of the cave eventually collapses. The old cave is now exposed to the sky. It leaves a nearly circular hole in the Earth's surface – a sinkhole!

Florida bedrock

Limestone is easily dissolved by acidic rain. Florida, USA, has lots of limestone and quite often gets sinkholes.

How deep can a sinkhole get?

Some of the largest sinkholes are underwater. These are called marine sinkholes. Dragon's Hole in the South China Sea is one such hole at over 300 m (984 ft) deep!

Ground caving in

Holes can form beneath the ground without people knowing. It's a total surprise when the ground collapses into a sinkhole!

Holey rock

Acidic rainwater dissolves some types of rock. This leaves holes in the rock and makes it weaker.

? Picture quiz

What caused the uneven land in Thailand?

See pages 132–133 for the answer

How do raindrops make a cave?

When it rains, some of the carbon dioxide gas in the air dissolves in the raindrops. This makes the water slightly acidic. When it meets certain rocks, such as limestone, the water eats away at them, making a hole. These holes grow and become caves.

Stalactite

If drops of water hang onto the ceiling of a cave for long enough, the minerals in the water can turn into rock. Over time, more drops make the rock grow down to create a stalactite.

Stalagmite

When water drips onto the cave floor, minerals dissolved in the water can become solid rock. These rocks grow up over time to make pointed stalagmites.

Can caves form in other ways?

Weathering

Rocks can be broken up physically, such as when ice freezes and melts in fractures. This can remove softer rock from below a harder one, leaving a cave.

Lava tubes

Lava tubes form when molten rock cools into stone around its edges. The lava in the centre remains hot, eventually flowing away and leaving a cave behind.

The front part of this cliff has been cut away to show the caves inside.

Column

If a stalactite and stalagmite meet, they fuse into a single pillar from floor to ceiling, called a column.

Fracture

Cracks or breaks in the ground, called fractures, let acidic water reach the rocks below.

? Quick quiz

1. Does a stalagmite grow from the floor or ceiling?

2. Is acid rain dangerous for humans?

3. What forms when a stalactite and stalagmite meet?

See pages 132–133 for the answers

Cave pool

Underground rivers and streams continue to dissolve the rock around them, and sometimes water collects in pools.

China

The plate beneath China is bordered by the Pacific and Indian plates. These rub and push against each other to cause earthquakes.

Turkey

Turkey's plate, Anatolia, is caught up between larger Eurasian and African plates. These plates are spinning and squishing Turkey!

Plate boundaries

When the edges of plates meet, this is called a plate boundary. Earthquakes often happen here.

Do earthquakes hit the same places?

Beneath the ground, the Earth's rocky crust is broken up into large pieces called tectonic plates. These plates constantly move and can rub against each other, pull apart, or collide to cause earthquakes.

USA

Earthquakes here happen mostly along the Pacific coast, where the North American plate slides past the Pacific one.

Ring of fire

The Pacific Ocean is the Earth's largest plate. Its boundaries are the site of many earthquakes.

Chile

Here, the Nazca plate slides beneath the South American plate. The most powerful earthquake ever recorded took place in Chile in 1960.

? Quick quiz

1. How do ocean ridges form?

2. Which plate is caught between the Eurasian and African plates?

3. The borders of which plate are known as the ring of fire?

See pages 132–133 for the answers

How do plates cause earthquakes?

Convergent

Plates collide. Volcanoes and mountains may form where continental and oceanic plates meet, or converge.

Transform

Plates slide past each other. When two plates rub against each other, it causes large earthquakes.

Divergent

Plates move apart. When this happens beneath oceans, molten rock rises and forms the sea floor.

Do islands float?

Islands don't really float, they just appear to! Islands are solidly attached to the ocean floor. They may form from the build-up of coral reefs on the seabed. Some are the tips of undersea volcanoes called seamounts.

Island

An island is a piece of land surrounded on all sides by water. Islands are always smaller than continents.

How are volcanic islands formed?

Lava from underwater volcanoes hardens into rock. The rock can build up in layers on the sides of the volcano. Eventually, the volcano peeps out of the sea.

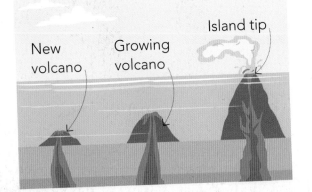

New volcano

Growing volcano

Island tip

Can you get floating rock islands?

One type of volcanic rock, pumice, is lighter than water, so it floats! Underwater volcanoes produce the rock and rafts of it float to look like islands.

? *True or false?*

1. A chain of islands is called an archipelago.

2. Pumice is the only known rock that floats in water.

See pages 132–133 for the answers

Rock beneath

Islands are anchored to the ocean floor deep below by a column of rock.

Sinking island

Giant plates, or segments, under the ocean floor can sink into the Earth. Any islands on top sink too!

Desert

This biome receives little or no rain. Here, tough plants and animals store water in their bodies and can cope with intense heat.

Dromedary camel

Saguaro cactus

Boreal forest, or taiga, is the largest biome on the Earth. Almost 30 per cent of the world's trees are found here.

Rainforest

Some rainforests get almost endless rain – up to 250 cm (98 in) a year! At least half of the plants and animals on the Earth live here.

How is a cactus like a camel?

A camel and a cactus can both go a long time without water, helping them to survive in their desert homes. Groups of living things that have features to help them cope with their environment are called biomes.

Grassland

Wide, treeless grasslands have plants that are adapted to a range of seasonal climate changes.

Polar regions

Lands near the North Pole and South Pole are cold all year round, and can be dry and lifeless. Life here is adapted to cold weather with little food.

Coniferous forest

Cold, semi-dry forests have trees with needle-like leaves. These stop moisture from escaping and minimize the effect of freezing temperatures.

Tundra

This semi-frozen world has few trees. Ice on the ground only melts during the short summer months.

Temperate forest

Broadleaf trees take advantage of more moisture, well-developed soils, and a climate that's not too hot or too cold.

Wetlands

These areas are covered by water all or part of the time. Animals here must adapt to a watery life, but be able to live on land too.

Are there other types of biome?

Farmland

The only human-made biome, farmland is made up of areas specially adapted by people to grow crops or rear animals.

Marine biomes

Land makes up just 29 per cent of the Earth's surface. The other 71 per cent is oceans and other water bodies, which we call marine biomes.

? Quick quiz

1. Which is the only human-made biome?

2. In which biome do camels live?

3. Which is the largest tropical rainforest in the world?

See pages 132–133 for the answers

Do swamp monsters exist?

There are some weird and wonderful creatures in swamps. A swamp is a forest that is fully or partially submerged in water. Swamp creatures in Florida, USA, have special features for living in water.

Swamp plants can be carnivorous! This means they eat insects and animals to survive.

Mangroves

These are trees that inhabit coastal saltwater swamps. Some mangroves have roots that jut out of the water to breathe.

Can people live in watery ecosystems?

People live in swamps by building houses on stilts. Many use airboats to get around. These have an aircraft-style propeller rather than an underwater one, which might get caught in shallow-water plants.

Florida softshell turtle

When a softshell turtle is underwater, it uses its long neck to stick its head above the surface to breathe.

West Indian manatee

Also called a "sea cow", this large animal grazes beneath the water in some swamps. It has flippers that help it swim through water.

American alligator

This reptile can grow up to 4.3 m (14 ft) long. An alligator can move quickly to drag prey underwater with its huge jaws.

Lesser siren

This looks like an eel but is actually a salamander. It has two legs and gills to breathe underwater like a fish!

Is there life on moss?

Tiny animals that are too small to see without a microscope live on moss. This plant forms a small habitat, which is a place where certain types of animal live. The moss helps the animals to survive in a number of ways.

Moss

Moss provides tiny creatures with leafy food, plenty of water to drink, and leaves to hide under when predators approach.

Mossy habitat

Moss often grows in areas with lots of water – for example, around forest streams. Moss keeps hold of the water, making it damp.

Nematodes

These tiny worms are found almost everywhere on the planet. They can even live in the soil beneath harsh deserts.

Bdelloid rotifers

Rotifers were around in the Earth's earliest days. They can dry themselves out and go into a kind of sleep to survive without water.

Tardigrades

These tiny animals might look cute but they eat rotifers, nematodes, and other tardigrades! Tardigrades are normally about 0.5 mm (0.02 in) long and can live for many years without water or food.

What is the biggest living thing on the Earth?

The world's largest living thing is an 80,000-year-old grove of Aspen trees in Utah, USA. The grove shares a single root system, and each tree is genetically identical to the next.

? Quick quiz

1. What is the name of an area where an animal lives?

2. What is the Earth's biggest living thing?

3. Which tiny creature is also known as a water bear?

See pages 132–133 for the answers

Blue planet

Much of the Earth is covered in water. Oceans, seas, lakes, and massive ice sheets all contain water. Water stored underground rises up to join rivers and can even shoot out of the ground as steam.

Why do things get carried out to sea?

Ocean water flows around the Earth in huge currents, which are like rivers. Gravity from the Moon and Sun pulls on seawater to make it move. Surface currents are driven largely by wind and can carry boats out to sea.

Windswept sea

Waves can travel around the world. They are formed by strong, persistent winds – or underwater earthquakes!

Wind currents

Wind travels in many different currents across the Earth's surface, such as in the westerlies and polar easterlies. These currents push the ocean's surface water along, creating movement.

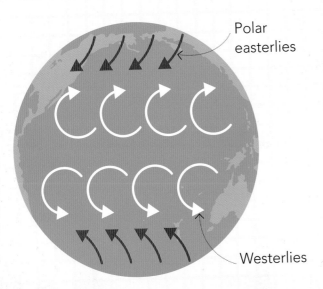

Polar easterlies

Westerlies

How do whirlpools form?

When surface currents collide, they force each other to turn and spin. Water rushes to fill the gap. This makes the whirlpool bigger. The stronger the currents, the more powerful the whirlpool's spin.

Direction of current

Cold, salty currents move away from the North and South Pole. Warm currents flow away from the Equator, which is around the middle of the Earth.

? True or false?

1. Ocean currents are driven partly by wind.

2. Ocean currents carry warm water from the North and South poles.

3. The westerlies are currents of water.

See pages 132–133 for the answers

Which waves can you surf?

Ocean waves are zones of rotating water. Surfers often wait for big waves that break, or fall forward. This reveals a smooth wall of rising water that can carry the surfer and their board.

? *True or false?*

1. Waves are columns of water.

2. Spilling waves are waves that break.

3. Tsunamis are giant waves caused by earthquakes.

See pages 132–133 for the answers

Do all waves break in the same way?

Spilling
When the tide is going out, or onshore winds blow, a gentle wave will form with foam spilling over the top.

Plunging
These waves occur when water hits an underwater obstruction or slope. The top of the wave is pushed up and tips over.

Collapsing
These are plunging waves that are not able to break over in a circular motion, but collapse instead.

Surging
These waves are wide and low in height. They move faster at the bottom than at the top.

Breaking wave
Waves approaching the shore drag along the rising ocean floor. This causes the waves to tilt and collaps

How a wave forms

Waves form as wind creates moving water. The water moves in columns of upright circles. The columns are pushed higher as the sea floor rises. The waves tilt forward to break.

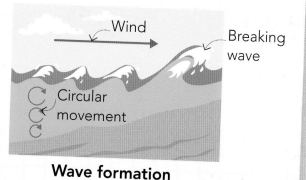

Wave formation

Wind direction

Waves travel in the direction of the wind that originally caused the water to move.

Surfing

Surfers ride the surface of the breaking wave. Waves that have travelled a long way are the most powerful.

Can we drink seawater?

Seawater is plentiful – over 71 per cent of all water on Earth is in the oceans! Saltwater, however, is not safe for humans to drink. It contains lots of dissolved salts and minerals, which are bad for us in large amounts. They can be removed in desalination plants to make it drinkable.

Filtering

The water is filtered to remove small particles of sand and algae, leaving only dissolved minerals.

Removal of debris

Seawater is sucked up from the ocean through pipes. First, any debris, such as seaweed, must be removed.

Saltwater

Many salts and minerals in seawater are washed into the oceans from the land. Seawater contains lots of sodium chloride – also known as table salt.

What can live in salty oceans?

Fish
The oceans contain more than 30,000 different species of fish! They drink a lot of seawater and get rid of extra salt using their gills.

Seaweed
Plant-like seaweed, such as kelp, can hide extra salt in special parts of their cells so the salt doesn't damage the seaweed.

Starfish
Starfish use seawater instead of blood. The insides of their cells are as salty as the seawater around them!

From salt to fresh
Next, the water is passed through a special membrane that allows water to cross it, but not the dissolved minerals.

Filter

RO membrane

Holding tank

? **Quick quiz**

1. What is sodium chloride also known as?

2. Is seawater or freshwater salty?

3. Can seawater freeze?

See pages 132–133 for the answers

Drinking water
Finally, chemicals are added to clean the water to make it safe to drink. Fresh water is transported to homes, factories, or farms.

Why does the Earth need the Moon?

The Moon has been the Earth's companion for 4.5 billion years. It formed from debris that broke off the Earth when a meteor smashed into the planet. The Earth would be very different without the Moon!

Frequent meteor strikes

The Moon pulls in space debris. This protects the Earth from some meteor strikes. With no Moon, the Earth would be hit by more meteors.

What else would happen without the Moon?

Shorter days

The Moon acts as a brake slowing the Earth's spin. Without it, the Earth would spin faster and days might only be five hours long!

Extreme weather

The Moon helps to control the seasons. Without the Moon, seasons could quickly change from very hot to bitterly cold.

No life

The Earth would have extreme weather and frequent meteor strikes without the Moon. This might have prevented early life from developing.

Brighter stars

The Sun reflects off the Moon at night to light up the sky. Dim stars blend into the light. A moonless night sky would show billions of stars.

Less wildlife activity at night

With nothing to reflect the Sun at night, animals that are awake at night would be unable to see.

How do tides happen?

The Moon pulls on oceans to cause them to bulge and swell, causing tides.

The Moon pulls on water as it circles the Earth.

Oceans facing the Moon

Tides also happen on the opposite side to the moon.

Oceans on the other side

Much smaller tides

The Moon is the main reason that tides move in and out. Without it, coastlines would be less worn away by tides.

Quick quiz

1. How old is the Moon?

2. Does the Earth's tilt change?

3. Which other body in space pulls on oceans to help cause tides?

See pages 132–133 for the answers

Where do rivers start?

Rivers flow from water sources such as melted mountain snow, underground streams, or high-up lakes. From here, they snake their way downhill to a lake, sea, or ocean. Rivers can cross entire continents!

Evidence of dried-up rivers has been found on the planet Mars!

Rhine River

This is the second largest river in Europe. It flows from the Alps through Austria, Germany, Switzerland, France, Liechtenstein, and the Netherlands.

What is the biggest river in the world?

The Amazon River in South America is the largest river on Earth. It carries almost twice the amount of water as the next largest river!

Headwaters

The source of a river is called its headwaters. The point where it reaches a lake, a sea, or an ocean is called the mouth.

Lake Toma

Lake Toma is a mountain lake in the Swiss Alps. It is thought to be the source of the Rhine River. Many lakes and streams lead to the Rhine. Lake Toma, however, is at the start of the river.

? True or false?

1. Headwaters are at the beginning of a river.

2. The Rhine is thought to begin at Lake Toma.

3. The longest river in the world is the Mississippi.

See pages 132–133 for the answers

Can a lake be bigger than a sea?

Lake Baikal in Siberia is bigger than Wales, UK, and three times the size of the smallest sea, the Sea of Marmara in Turkey. Lakes and seas are surrounded by land. However, seas are connected to oceans.

Freshwater lake

Most lakes contain fresh water. This is saltless water from inland sources such as rivers.

How are seas different from oceans?

Seas are salty because they are connected to the oceans. Oceans are huge bodies of water that are not surrounded by land.

Lake or sea?

Bodies of water such as the Dead Sea in the Middle East are salty, but are considered lakes because they don't link to an ocean. The Caspian Sea is a lake in western Asia that once connected to an ocean.

andlocked

Most lakes, including Lake Baikal, are landlocked, or surrounded by land. • • • • •

Lake Baikal contains over 22 per cent of the Earth's freshwater!

The Caspian Sea

? Quick quiz

1. Is the Dead Sea a sea?

2. Do lakes connect to an ocean?

3. Which is the smallest sea?

See pages 132–133 for the answers

Where is the biggest waterfall?

Where is it?
The Denmark Strait is a channel of the Atlantic Ocean located between Greenland and Iceland.

The biggest waterfall on Earth is under the ocean. All water on the Earth's surface flows downwards, due to gravity. The Denmark Strait cataract is over three times the size of the tallest waterfall above ground!

Warm surface water
Water near the surface of the ocean is warmed by the Sun. This makes it less dense, or lighter, than colder water below.

Strong current
The rapid movement of the heavier bottom flow, or current, sculpts and reshapes the Atlantic Ocean floor.

? Quick quiz

1. In which ocean is the Denmark Strait?

2. Which is the tallest waterfall on land?

3. Which is the tallest waterfall in the world?

See pages 132–133 for the answers

Ocean floor

Greenland

Denmark Strait

Iceland

Which are the biggest land waterfalls?

Angel Falls
This waterfall in Venezuela is the tallest on land. It falls 979 m (3,211 ft) in two drops to the valley below.

Khone Falls
The world's widest waterfall is in Laos. Khone Phapheng Falls is a staggering 10,783 m (35,376 ft) wide!

3,505 m
(11,500 ft)

Cold water overflow
An underwater river of cold water cascades over a giant underwater ridge in the Denmark Strait cataract.

Water sinks
Water cools as it flows northwards near the Arctic Circle. This makes it denser, or heavier. It sinks to the ocean floor and joins a current flowing over the cataract.

What is the biggest body of ice on Earth?

Ice sheet

The Antarctic ice sheet is a layer of ice that covers the continent of Antarctica. It is the largest body of ice on Earth. Its ice moves into the Lambert-Fisher Glacier, a huge, slow-moving river of ice.

Floating ice

The largest floating body of ice on Earth is the Ross ice shelf. It is over 800,000 km (500,000 miles) wide, which is almost the same size as the US state of California!

How big are icebergs?

The bit of an iceberg that you can see above water is only a tiny part of the whole thing. Icebergs are floating chunks of ice that have broken off glaciers or huge, floating ice shelves. Icebergs can be mountain-sized!

Location

Most icebergs break off from Greenland's glaciers or Antarctica's ice sheets. From here, they can travel hundreds of kilometres.

Size

A chunk of ice has to be 5 m (16 ft) wide to be called an iceberg. Smaller ice chunks in the ocean are called bergy bits or growlers.

Underwater bulk

Around 90 per cent of an iceberg is hidden below the water. This is because it is too heavy to float entirely above the surface. Ice is about 10 per cent less dense than water is!

The largest iceberg ever recorded was 295 km (183 miles) wide!

Quick quiz

1. What is the biggest body of ice on the Earth?

2. How much of an iceberg is underwater?

3. What is a growler?

See pages 132–133 for the answers

How is a glacier like a cheese grater?

Glaciers are like rivers of ice that slowly move over land. Glaciers carve out bits of ground just like the sharp edges of a cheese grater breaking off bits of cheese. The biggest glaciers are found in Antarctica and Greenland.

Glacial grooves

When rocks or sharp ice in the glacier drag through rock and soil, they create grooves. This is similar to how a cheese grater carves grooves into cheese!

Glacier

Glaciers are rivers of ice that form when snow builds up faster than it can melt. The snow compacts over time to form a block of ice.

Movement

Glaciers move at different speeds. This can range from 0.5 m (1.6 ft) to 30 m (98 ft) a day!

Broken rocks

Small rocks and even boulders sometimes get picked up by glaciers and carried away. These are called "erratics".

What else do melted glaciers leave behind?

Eskers

Eskers are long, winding ridges of sand and gravel left behind when glaciers melt.

Moraines

These are deposits of till, or rock and soil, that occur along the edges of a melting glacier.

Till

Glacial till is the sediment left behind when a glacier melts, and is made up of fine dust and small rocks.

? Quick quiz

1. What is an esker?

2. Do glaciers move?

3. What's the biggest glacier on the Earth?

See pages 132–133 for the answers

What's at the bottom of the ocean?

There are parts of the ocean that are less explored than the nearby areas of our Solar System! However, some parts have been reached by robotic or crewed craft. Here, you might find volcanoes, coral reefs, or shipwrecks.

Sunken city

Oceans rise and fall ov time, as ice sheets mel land sinks, or volcanoe erupt. The rising water can cover ancient cities

Coral reefs

They might look like plants, but corals are actually animals! They have limestone skeletons and form communities in shallow water.

Shipwreck

Weather, underwater hazards, or war may cause ships to sink in the ocean. Sea creatures often make their home here.

Pillow basalt

Young, pillowy basalt rocks can be found lining the ocean's floor. These are some of the newest rocks on the planet.

The ocean's deepest point is 10,916 m (35,814 ft), or nearly one and a quarter Mount Everests, deep!

The five oceans

One big body of water covers more than 70 per cent of the Earth's surface! There are five oceans within this giant body of water. These are the Atlantic, Pacific, Indian, Arctic, and Southern.

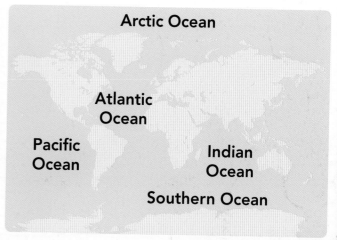

Arctic Ocean

Atlantic Ocean

Pacific Ocean

Indian Ocean

Southern Ocean

Mid-ocean ridge

These are underwater mountain ranges. New ocean crust is created from molten rock that bubbles up and hardens.

Hydrothermal vents

Openings bring superheated water from cracks stretching deep into the Earth.

Underwater volcano

Volcanoes can form above cracks in the ocean floor. Molten rock rises and hardens in layers to form cone shapes.

Submarine cable

Long, underwater cables connect telephones and carry WiFi internet between continents.

Where is the ocean's twilight zone?

Below the ocean's surface are zones, or layers, of water. The deeper these get, the darker and colder they become. The twilight zone is the semi-dark second layer. Very different types of creatures live in each zone.

? Quick quiz

1. What is bioluminescence?

2. Which ocean zone do seahorses live in?

3. Do giant squids exist?

See pages 132–133 for the answers

Killer whale

Sea turtle

Chain catshark

Lanternfish

Swordfish

Seahorse

Hammerhead shark

Seal

Sunlit zone
0 to 200 m (0 to 656 ft)
Sunlight easily reaches the many creatures in this shallow zone.

Twilight zone
200 to 1,000 m (656 to 3,280 ft)
Less sunlight reaches the water in this zone. It is darker and colder than the zone above because of the lack of sunlight.

Midnight zone

1,000 to 4,000 m (3,280 to 13,123 ft)

All sunlight is absorbed by the water above, creating a dark and cold world. Some animals make their own light.

Footballfish

Tiburonia jellyfish

Dumbo octopus

Frilled shark

Barreleye

Abyss

4,000 to 6,000 m (13,123 to 19,685 ft)

Pressure from the water above pushes down on fish. It is freezing cold.

Hagfish

Tripod fish

Sea pig

Hadal

Below 6,000 m (19,685 ft)

Few creatures can survive here due to the total darkness and massive pressure from the water above.

Giant tube worm

Giant amphipod

How do deep-sea fish find food?

Bioluminescence

Creatures of the deep ocean use chemicals in their bodies to create light, called bioluminescence.

Expandable stomachs

Some deep-sea fish have large jaws and stomachs that expand to eat fish bigger than them.

Up in the air

The weather is different around the world and changes from season to season. Rain and lightning form inside clouds that float across the sky. Powerful winds cause amazing weather spectacles, such as microbursts, hurricanes, and tornadoes.

Is there air in space?

Air in the Earth's atmosphere contains tiny particles of gas. You breathe in billions of these with one breath. There are fewer gas particles the higher up you go. Space begins where gas particles are too few and far apart to make air we can breathe.

Solar wind flows through space from the Sun. It is plasma, which is like a hot gas, glowing with energy.

How is air different from space?

Particles of gas are more closely packed together in air than they are in space. We breathe in a gas called oxygen to survive, which makes up around 21 per cent of the air.

Air particles   **Particles in space**

Particles

Gas particles in space are so far apart that it is nearly a vacuum, or empty space.

How does a spacecraft fly?

Modern spacecraft

Superheated gases expand from burning fuel inside modern rockets. This pushes the rocket forwards.

Future rockets

Future rockets may use light itself as fuel. This would be converted into energy to move the craft forward.

Flying the flag

It looks like there is wind blowing this flag, but the flag is hanging from a rod along the top! The Moon has no atmosphere, just like space.

? Quick quiz

1. What is solar wind?
   a) Air blowing in space
   b) Plasma from the Sun
   c) A spacecraft powered by the Sun

2. Why does the flag look like it's blowing on the Moon?
   a) It is blowing in the wind
   b) The astronaut is blowing it
   c) There's a secret rod along the top that holds it up

See pages 132–133 for the answers

Why are there colours in the sky?

The sky can change colour from blue to dusky red because of sunlight. Light is made up of different colours. The air breaks this up, or scatters it, into separate colours in the sky.

? Quick quiz

1. Which colour is most easily scattered by the air?

2. How many colours of the rainbow are there?

3. What colour are dusty skies?

See pages 132–133 for the answers

Blue sky

A clear blue sky is the normal colour as light enters the atmosphere. This is because blue light is most easily scattered by the air.

Yellow sky

When smoky, hazy, or dusty skies occur, light is scattered into yellowy orange colours.

How rainbows are formed

Sunlight contains all the colours of the rainbow. When it rains, raindrops in the air bend the light. This separates the light out into all of its colours.

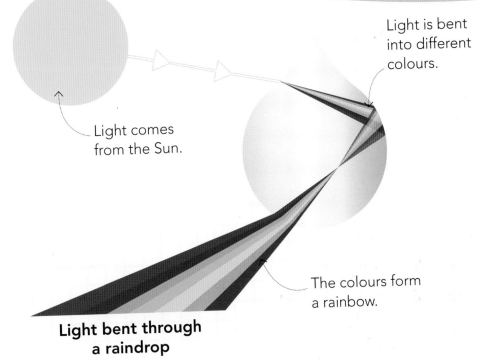

Light comes from the Sun.

Light is bent into different colours.

The colours form a rainbow.

Light bent through a raindrop

Sunset

As the sun sets, its light must pass through the atmosphere sideways. Light is scattered into brilliant reds, yellows, and oranges.

Why do we have seasons?

It takes a year for the Earth to orbit (circle) the Sun. During this time, the Sun's energy gives us warmth and light. However, the Earth is tilted. Parts of the Earth get more or less energy as they tilt towards or away from the Sun. This creates the seasons.

Summer

During summer, your half of the Earth is tilted towards the Sun. Summers are typically hot, and days are long.

New Yo[...]
City, US[...]

?

Quick quiz

1. How many days does it take the Earth to orbit the Sun?

2. Do all animals hibernate?

3. Do seasons take place at the same time around the Earth?

See pages 132–133 for the answers

Autumn

This season takes place when your half of the Earth begins to tilt away from the Sun. The leaves on many trees change colour.

Spring

We experience spring when our half of the Earth begins to tilt towards the Sun. The weather turns warmer and plants blossom.

The Earth's axis

Winter

When the half of the Earth you live on is tilted away from the Sun, winter occurs. Winters are typically cold and the days are short.

How do seasons affect animals?

Hibernation

Many animals cannot find food during the cold winter months. They go into a deep sleep, or hibernate, until spring comes.

Migration

Some animals just get up and move when the weather gets cold! There are some birds that fly to warmer places in the winter months.

Winter coats

Many animals change their bodies in winter. They get thicker, warmer coats. Arctic hares turn white to hide in snow!

Why are places hot or cold?

Sunlight does not strike the Earth evenly, so some places receive more of its heat than others. This creates hot or cold areas, called climate zones. Other things affect temperature too.

Boreal

Boreal, or taiga, climates have very long, cold winters and short, cool summers. They are typically found towards the top of the Earth, in places such as Canada or Siberia in Russia.

Tropical

The tropics are just north and south of the equator, in the equatorial zone. They are typically hot regions, and can be very dry or steamy!

Hot equator

The equator is the area around the middle of the Earth. It gets the most direct sunlight and is one of the hottest areas on our planet.

Axis

Equator

Sun

Earth

Mountain climate

High-up places such as mountains are cold. The air gets thinner and colder as you move higher up into the atmosphere.

Temperate

Areas between the tropics and the polar regions are known as temperate zones. Here, temperatures change between cold and warm seasons.

How does the Gulf Stream affect the climate?

This is a current of warm water that flows in the North Atlantic Ocean. It brings warm tropical waters northwards.

Mediterranean

Lands around the Mediterranean Sea have hot, dry summers and cool, often wet winters. These areas rarely get very cold, as they are warmed all year round by the nearby sea.

? Picture quiz

Why is Mount Kilimanjaro icy if it is in Tanzania on the hot equator?

See pages 132–133 for the answer

Climate zone key

- Polar
- Boreal
- Mountain
- Temperate
- Mediterranean
- Arid
- Tropical

Arid

Arid, or dry, climates contain grasslands or deserts that receive very little rainfall. Deserts can be extremely hot during the day and cold at night.

Polar

These zones at the top and bottom of the Earth are the coldest places. They receive the least sunlight of any part of the planet.

Why does water fall from the sky?

The Sun heats liquid water on the ground. This turns the water into a gas, which rises. High up in the sky, the gas cools down to form water droplets and ice crystals. These fall to the Earth when they become too heavy.

What is evaporation?

Liquid water becomes a gas called water vapour when it is heated or changes pressure. This process is called evaporation. In nature, the Sun's heat turns the water into vapour.

Water vapour

Liquid water

Heat

Water vapour

Liquid water becomes a gas in warm sunlight or when the air pressure decreases due to wind. Water vapour becomes part of the air.

How do people study rain and snow?

Meteorologists study the weather. They use radar to look at liquid water and ice inside clouds, called precipitation.

Water

Rain tops up liquid water sources such as rivers.

Clouds

he air gets colder
gher up. Water vapour
ondenses, or cools down,
form water droplets.
hese produce clouds.

Rain

Tiny water droplets in clouds get bigger as more droplets join them. They become too heavy and fall as rain.

There is the same amount of water on the Earth now as when oceans first formed, 3.8 billion years ago.

? Quick quiz

1. What is the name of the process in which a liquid turns into a gas when it is heated but not boiled?

2. What is water vapour?

3. What are scientists that study the weather called?

See pages 132–133 for the answers

How are clouds different?

Structure

Is a cloud billowy and tall, or thin and wispy? The structure, or make-up, helps us know what weather to expect.

Altitude

Wind speed, temperature, and pressure change with altitude, or height. This creates different types of cloud.

Precipitation

Water falling as snow, rain, or ice is called precipitation. Clouds that carry precipitation look different.

Is that a dinosaur in the clouds?

Clouds form when water vapour in the sky cools and condenses, or turns into ice or water droplets. These puffs of grey or white form many shapes and have different names.

Cirrus

These are the highest clouds. They are thin and wispy. Cirrus form from thin sheets of ice crystals.

Cirrocumulus

A type of cirrus cloud, these form close-together patterns that are often stripy.

Altostratus

This is a thin layer of cloud in middle altitudes. It is usually a mix of liquid

12,000 m
39,370 ft

11,000 m
36,090 ft

10,000 m
32,810 ft

9,000 m
29,530 ft

8,000 m

These are thick layers of mostly joined-up clouds. They can cause drizzly days.

Cumulus

A puffy, low cloud is called a cumulus. These rise above updrafts of hot air in the summer heat.

Dinosaur cloud

Cumulus clouds or other types can form odd shapes that inspire the imagination – such as dinosaurs.

Cumulonimbus

This is a massively tall, sometimes scary-looking, storm cloud that is usually flat at the top like an anvil.

Stratus

These low clouds form a flat-bottomed layer that may blanket the sky.

? Quick quiz

1. What are the highest clouds called?

2. What is water falling from clouds, such as rain or snow, called?

3. What is a tall, flat-topped storm cloud called?

See pages 132–133 for the answers

22,970 ft

6,000 m
19,690 ft

5,000 m
16,400 ft

4,000 m
13,120 ft

3,000 m
9,840 ft

2,000 m
6,560 ft

1,000 m
3,280 ft

Sea level

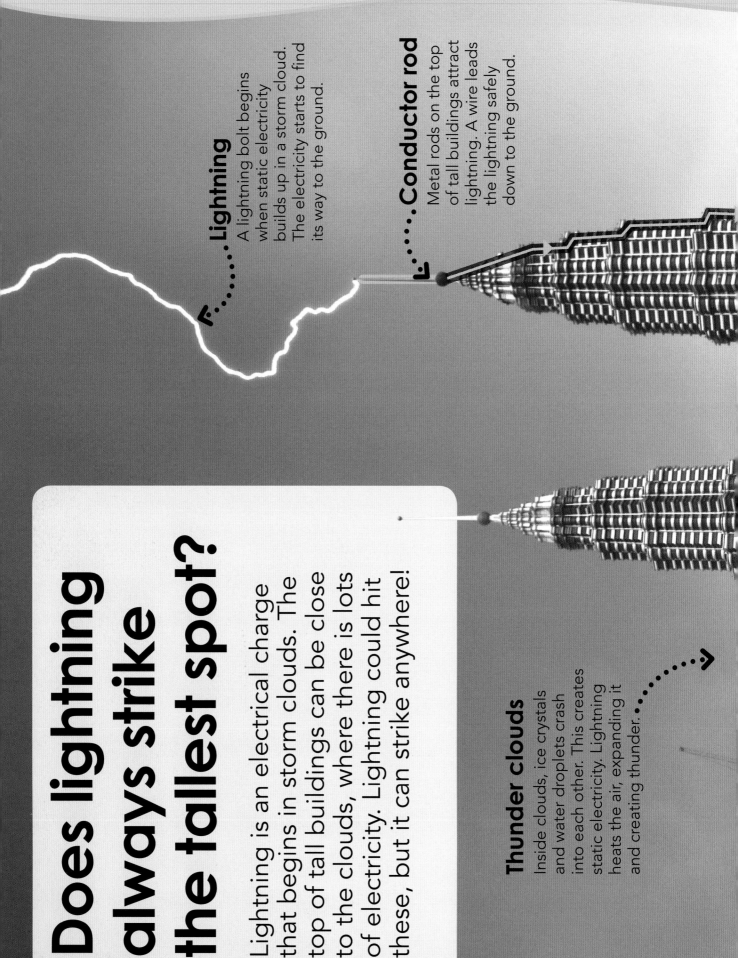

Does lightning always strike the tallest spot?

Lightning is an electrical charge that begins in storm clouds. The top of tall buildings can be close to the clouds, where there is lots of electricity. Lightning could hit these, but it can strike anywhere!

Lightning
A lightning bolt begins when static electricity builds up in a storm cloud. The electricity starts to find its way to the ground.

Conductor rod
Metal rods on the top of tall buildings attract lightning. A wire leads the lightning safely down to the ground.

Thunder clouds
Inside clouds, ice crystals and water droplets crash into each other. This creates static electricity. Lightning heats the air, expanding it and creating thunder.

Earthing rod

The lightning is carried to a rod in the ground. This stops it from damaging the building.

How does lightning make rocks?

When lightning hits sand, such as on a beach, it heats the grains. This melts them into glass, and makes beautiful forms called fulgurites.

? True or false?

1. Lightning can strike anywhere.

2. Thunder is the sound of air that has been heated by lightning.

3. Lightning grows from static electricity.

See pages 132–133 for the answers

Can humans make it rain?

Technology has been used to try to turn water droplets and ice crystals inside clouds into rain or snow. This process is called cloud seeding. It has been used to increase snowfall in some places. However, some scientists think it does not work very well.

Aerial seeder

Aircraft carry machines that inject chemicals into clouds. These chemicals could be ba for the environment.

What is a microburst?

Microbursts are huge, natural downdrafts of wind caused by the sudden cooling of air high in the atmosphere. The rush of winds can cause damage to aircraft.

Table salt can be used to seed clouds. It causes water droplets to join together as raindrops.

Clouds

Clouds that contain lots of water droplets and ice crystals are often the targets of seeding.

Seeding

Different chemicals are used. Some attract water droplets, which join together to form rain. Others attract ice crystals to form large snowflakes.

? Quick quiz

1. Which household substance can be used to seed clouds?

2. Can we make it rain without clouds?

3. What joins together to form rain?

See pages 132–133 for the answers

How does a tornado form?

Tornadoes are rotating columns of air that can spin at speeds of over 482 kph (300 mph)! The air beneath some storms can begin to rise and spin to form a mesocyclone. If a downward flow of air forms next to the mesocyclone, a tornado can develop.

Tornado

A downward draft of air can form next to the rising air. Tornadoes often occur when this happens.

How do we measure the strength of tornadoes?

In the USA, tornadoes are ranked from zero to five on the Enhanced Fujita (EF) scale.

EF-0 tornado

An EF-0 tornado is the weakest, causing minimal damage. It has the lowest wind speeds of any tornado.

EF-5 tornado

These tornadoes are the most powerful. EF-5s can be 1.6 km (1 mile) wide and destroy most things in their path.

Spinning air

Tornadoes form beneath parent storm clouds. Rising air starts to spin high above the ground.

Dusty base

The tornado pulls in dust, debris, and other objects in its path. This gives it a brown or grey colour.

What is a hurricane?

Also called tropical cyclones, hurricanes are spinning storm clouds that form over some parts of the ocean. Hurricanes that reach land can cause a huge amount of damage.

Eye of
the storm

Spiral
clouds

Surface winds

Ocean

? Quick quiz

1. Which scale measures the strength of tornadoes?

2. What type of storm cloud might tornadoes form beneath?

3. What is the centre of a hurricane called?

See pages 132–133 for the answers

Living on the Earth

The number of humans on the Earth has continued to grow throughout history. Our planet provides water, food, air to breathe, and fuel to create energy. We have changed the Earth in many ways, and need to make sure we take care of it.

How many people live on the Earth?

At the last count, there were more than 7.5 billion people on the Earth. If we all stood next to each other in a line, it would stretch around the world more than 88 times! We need to make sure there are enough resources, such as food and water, for everyone.

Overpopulation

The population of the Earth is growing. There are only enough natural resources for about 10 billion people.

Which natural resources are essential for human survival?

Food

Most food is grown on farms and transported to shops. Scientists are researching other ways to get food in case we run out of space to farm.

Water

Clean water is hard to get in areas where there aren't lakes or rivers. Water can't be made, so we have to share what's there.

Tokyo

Japan's capital, Tokyo, is one of the world's largest cities. There are almost 15,000 people per square km (0.6 square mile).

World population

Every country in the world has a different sized population. Some populations are growing at a fast rate. Others, such as Japan, are actually shrinking.

World population by continent

Key

Most populated   Least populated

? Quick quiz

1. How many people can the world's natural resources support?

2. Is the world's population growing?

3. What is the capital of Japan?

See pages 132–133 for the answers

How do countries begin?

For hundreds of thousands of years, humans have lived in tribes. Over time, these groups grew and combined. People moved to new areas and developed their own cultures and governments, eventually forming countries.

Colonies

Throughout history, people have always travelled from one country to another. Sometimes these people claimed the new land as their own, but they often took land from people already living there.

Virginian Governor's Palace, USA

North America

South America

Antarctica

? Quick quiz

1. What is the oldest country that exists today?

2. Which mountain range separates France and Spain?

3. Which country controlled almost a quarter of the world in the 1900s?

See pages 132–133 for the answers

Explored land

Early humans explored the Earth by land and by sea. The first humans arrived in South America over 15,000 years ago.

Cartagena, Colombia

Conquered land

Many countries have fought wars to gain land or resources from other countries. In the early 1900s, Britain controlled almost a quarter of the world.

Pyrenees, France

Natural boundaries

Landforms, such as mountain ranges, deserts, rivers, and oceans, can form barriers that separate distinct cultures. Many of these features create borders between countries.

Europe

Asia

Africa

Farms along the Nile, Egypt

Farming together

Early people lived together in settlements to produce food. Farming meant people could stay in one place, rather than moving around to hunt.

Island countries

Islands are often isolated and develop into single countries with the ocean surrounding them. Both Australia and New Zealand are "island" countries.

Australasia

What makes a country unique?

Languages

Languages allow people to communicate. They may change over time as new words are invented.

Religion

Religions provide a set of beliefs around which people gather together. Countries may have one main religion, or many.

Culture

Culture is the art, beliefs, language, and traditions of a people that develops over time. It makes each country unique.

How have we changed the Earth?

Humans live on every continent and have changed the surface of the Earth forever. We use many natural resources, shape the land, and build huge cities.

? **Picture quiz**

What is this ancient creature that was hunted to extinction by humans?

See pages 132–133 for the answer

Dammed lake

The O'Shaughnessy Dam in California, USA, created the Hetch Hetchy reservoir. It flooded a whole valley with water.

River valley

Damming a river changes the landscape dramatically. The lake created behind a dam floods the ground and covers trees.

Before

After

How else have we affected the Earth?

Farming
We have built farms over large areas of the Earth's surface to raise animals and grow crops, such as rice. Forests are often cleared to make space for farms, and rivers are diverted to water crops.

Deforestation
Forests are cut down to clear land for farms and cities, and to produce wood for building or fuel. Without trees, soil can wash away and the land can become desert.

> Over 83 per cent of land on the Earth has been changed by humans.

Modern city
Cities can be huge and produce lots of waste. Tall skyscrapers change the skyline, like those in Panama City, Panama.

rowing town
en small towns change the land ound them. Farms are built to grow od, the course of rivers can be anged to provide water, and forests e cut down to make space for houses.

Before

After

What is a city?

Cities are places where large groups of people live close together. In cities, people often have access to useful services such as hospitals, schools, and shops.

Education

City governments will often be in charge of schools. Universities provide education for older students.

Religion

Places where people can practise religion such as cathedrals have always been a major part of city life.

Shops

Cities may have first started so that people could trade, or swap, goods. Modern cities have shops that sell goods.

Berlin, Germany

How tall can a building be?

Currently being built in Saudi Arabia, the Jeddah Tower will open in 2020. It will be the tallest building ever, at over 1 km (0.6 miles) high.

1,008 m (3,307 ft)

632 m (2,073 ft)

368 m (1,207 ft)

Jeddah Tower

Shanghai Tower

Berlin T Tower

Health and safety

City hospitals help provide health care for people. Ambulances zip through the air and on the ground to take people to hospital.

Berlin TV Tower

Public transport

Different forms of transport such as buses, rental bikes, underground trains, and trams allow many people to travel quickly around a city.

Government

Cities are managed by governments. Their job can include keeping people safe by enforcing laws to stop bad behaviour.

Have there always been cities?

Cities may date back to as far as 10,000 years ago. Cities grew from towns, which were likely begun so that groups of people could better protect themselves and trade, or swap, goods with others.

? Picture quiz

According to legend, which twins built the city of Rome in Italy?

See pages 132–133 for the answer

How do we feed everyone?

Keeping the billions of people on the Earth alive requires a lot of food! Many groups of people rely on wheat to make bread and pasta. This is grown in places with the right climate and soils and sent around the world.

Wheat

Wheat grains are separated from the stalks. The grain is stored in tall buildings called silos to protect it from insects and rain.

Staple crops

Wheat, maize, soya beans, and rice are staple crops available around the world. These are grown in places with the right soils and climates.

Maize

Soya bean

Rice

Combine harvester

Machines help us produce lots of food. Combines are used to collect much more wheat than people can gather by hand.

See pages 132–133 for the answers

? Quick quiz

1. Which crop is usually used to make bread?

2. Which machine is often used to gather wheat?

3. What is the farming of animals also known as?

China, India, Russia, and the USA are the largest producers of food crops in the world.

Wheatfield

ast fields of wheat can be een in Kansas, USA. Around e world, wheat is used to ake flour for pasta, bread, nd cakes.

How else do we get food?

Fishing
Fishing is a major source of food for regions bordering bodies of water. Fish, shrimp, and other marine life are often farmed in oceans, lakes, and rivers.

Animal farming
Animal husbandry is the farming of animals for food stock. Cows, pigs, chickens, and other animals are raised for their meat.

Gathering
Early humans gathered nuts, berries, and fruit in the wild. The finding and gathering of these foods still occurs today.

How do we find our way around?

To find our way around a new place, we need to know where we are, and where everything else is. Maps describe the area around us. The pictures match up with real-life features that we can spot as we explore.

Roads

White or black lines on map usually show road. The thicker the line, the bigger the road.

Rivers

Blue lines show rivers and waterways. If you need to get somewhere by a blue line, look out for a river!

Compass bearings

A compass shows the direction you're going in, be it north, east, south, or west. The north arrow points towards the Earth's magnetic North Pole.

Terrains

The shape of a landscape is called its terrain. Curved lines on map called contours, show hills.

Colours

Different colours on a map often match up to the feature they're showing. If you're by a grassy area, look for green!

What are longitude and latitude?

Equator

Meridian line

Latitude is your distance north or south of the Earth's equator. Longitude is how far you are either east or west of Europe's meridian line.

Symbols

Pictures, or symbols, are used to show important features. A train station might be indicated by a train symbol, for example.

? True or false?

1. The prime meridian line runs through Europe.

2. North is the direction towards the bottom of the Earth.

3. Terrain is shown by pictures of trains.

See pages 132–133 for the answers

Landmarks

Areas have unique places, or landmarks. Maps often show these so that you can find them easily.

Some scientists think there will be more plastic in the oceans than fish by 2050!

Loose litter

Rainwater can carry plastic from bins or other rubbish sites into rivers, which lead into the ocean.

Plastic pollution

Plastic is used to make everything from aeroplane part to food packaging. Lots of this ends up in oceans.

How much plastic is in the ocean?

Millions of tonnes of plastic makes its way into our oceans each year. Lots of this comes from food or drink packaging. We can help reduce the amount of plastic in oceans by using fewer plastic items, or by recycling them.

Microplastics

Plastics in the ocean eventually break down into smaller bits. Seawater contains billions of these tiny pieces of plastic.

Why is plastic bad for oceans?

Harmful to wildlife

Wildlife can get caught up in plastic. This makes it hard for the animal to find food or escape predators.

Plastic food

Sealife can accidentally eat tiny bits of ocean plastic, called microplastics. Plastic found in sealife could be harmful to humans who eat it.

Great Pacific Garbage Patch

A huge patch of plastic can be found in the Pacific Ocean. It is around three times the size of France and contains about 80,000 tonnes (88,185 tons) of floating waste!

Rubbish is pulled into patches by rotating currents, called gyres.

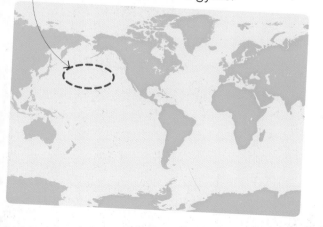

? Quick quiz

1. How much does the plastic in the Great Pacific Garbage Patch weigh?

2. What are rotating ocean currents called?

See pages 132–133 for the answers

What is recycling?

If you recycle something, it gets turned into a new object. Many of the natural materials we use to make things will one day run out. Recycling human-made items means they don't go to waste. Here's how it works.

Bales

The plastic is crushed and made into blocks called bales.

Sorting

Materials that can be recycled first need to be sorted into their different types. Plastics, glass, and cardboard are all recycled separately.

Recyclable plastic is separated from other types of recycling.

Some, but not all, plastics can be recycled.

Plastic pellets

PET pellets can be melted down and poured into moulds to make new objects, such as bottles.

Plastic bottles

A material called polyethylene terephthalate, or PET, is found in most plastic bottles. This can be used to make new plastic objects.

See pages 132–133 for the answers

Flakes

The bales are chopped up into small flakes of plastic.

The melted PET hardens into a lump and is cut into pellets.

Cleaning

Water separates the PET from the parts of the bottle that can't be recycled. The heavy PET sinks. Labels and other bits that can't be recycled float upwards.

Melting and chopping

The PET flakes are melted. The liquid plastic hardens into a lump. The lump is chopped into pellets.

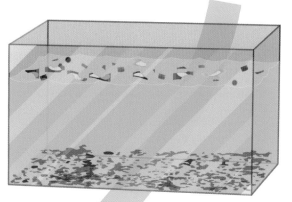

? True or false?

1. All materials can be recycled.

2. Materials that can be recycled need to be recycled by type.

3. PET is a recyclable material found in plastics.

What else can be recycled?

Paper

Paper rubbish is mashed up with water and heated. This mixture is strained and rolled out into new paper.

Metal

Metal that can be recycled is cleaned and heated until it melts. The liquid metal is then poured into bar-shaped moulds. The metal cools and hardens into bars that can be shaped into new objects.

How bad is a drought?

We call a long, rainless period a drought. When a drought occurs, it can cause problems for plants, animals, and people. Droughts usually happen in dry areas and can last for many years.

Wildfire

Dry winds fuel wildfires. These spread quickly through dried-out trees in forests.

It didn't rain for 14 years in Arica, Chile, between 1903 and 1918!

Dust storm

Rain sticks soil together and stops it from blowing away. Without rain, soil loosens into dust and is blown into huge clouds by the wind.

Parched land

Without moisture from rain, soils crack and harden in the sun. The land becomes a dry, almost lifeless desert.

Crop failure

Crops need water to survive. In a drought, water sources can run out because they aren't replenished. This means farmers can't keep their crops alive.

Dust devil

Rapidly rising air from drought-hit land that has been heated by the Sun pulls in dirt and dust. This forms mini-cyclones called dust devils that roam the countryside.

? Quick quiz

1. What was the Dust Bowl?
   a) A giant bowl of dust
   b) A drought in Australia
   c) Drought-hit 1930s Southern High Plains of the USA

2. What is a dust devil?
   a) A type of coyote
   b) A mini-cyclone
   c) Smoke from a wildfire

See pages 132–133 for the answers.

How can we save water during a drought?

Take shorter showers

The average shower uses the same amount of water as 270 glasses of the stuff!

Farm fewer animals

Cows drink up to 20 times the amount of water that humans do. If we raised fewer cows for meat, we'd save a lot of water.

Is the Earth getting warmer?

The Earth's climate changes naturally over time. The planet has been warmer, and colder, in the past. We live in a relatively cool period today, but human activity is causing temperatures to rise.

20,000 years ago

Around 2.6 million years ago, the Earth began to cool. The ice that covered a lot of the planet only began to melt 20,000 years ago.

120 years ago

The growth of factories increased the amount of greenhouse gases being released into the air, further warming the planet

56 million years ago

The Earth was quite hot in the past! About 56 million years ago, the Earth was so warm there was no ice at the North Pole!

7°C (12.6°F)
warmer than now

5°C (9°F)
colder than now

1°C (1.8°F)
colder than no

Greenhouse gases

The atmosphere acts like a greenhouse. The Sun warms the Earth and the atmosphere traps some of the heat. Certain gases, called greenhouse gases, trap extra heat.

The Sun heats the Earth.

Greenhouse gases in the air trap more heat.

The atmosphere traps the heat.

resent day

e Earth is getting armer. Greenhouse ases from vehicles nd power plants peed up natural arming. Awareness helping bring bout cleaner air.

Picture quiz

?

Which planet has a thick atmosphere of greenhouse gases?

See pages 132–133 for the answer

80 years in the future

The Earth may become warmer than today. Areas of ice may have melted into the oceans. This extra water could flood coastal areas.

Current temperature

3°C (5.4°F) warmer than now

Oxygen

Humans need to breathe in a gas called oxygen to survive. Trees release oxygen into the air.

Carbon dioxide

Trees take in a gas called carbon dioxide out of the air. This gas traps heat. Too much of it can make the Earth hotter.

How do trees help humans?

Trees help create the oxygen that we need in order to survive. Their roots take in water from the ground, which stops flooding. They can even increase the amount of rain in an area because the water evaporates from their leaves.

? Quick quiz

1. What gas do trees release into the air?

2. What is the name of the process in which plants make glucose?

See pages 132–133 for the answers

How can eating insects save trees?

Forests are chopped down to make way for farmland. This is used to raise animals for meat. Some people choose to eat foods that aren't produced using lots of land, such as insects.

Photosynthesis

Plants make their own food through a process called photosynthesis. They use sunlight, carbon dioxide, and water to make a type of sugar called glucose. Oxygen is also made and released into the air.

Sun

Plants breathe in carbon dioxide.

Sunlight is absorbed.

Oxygen is released.

Roots pull in water.

The human effect

When we burn fuel in cars or to power electricity plants, it produces carbon dioxide.

What is the future of energy?

Power plants that create electricity have mainly burned fossil fuels up to this time. Supplies of these fuels, such as crude oil, will become harder to find. Carbon dioxide is produced when fossil fuels burn, making the Earth warmer. People are slowly switching to different, less damaging, ways to make electricity.

Wind energy

Large windmills contain turbines used to create electricity. Most turbines are on land, but they can also be built in the ocean.

Tidal energy

The movement of oceans in tides can be used to generate, or make, energy.

Every 10 seconds, enough crude oil to fill an Olympic swimming pool is taken out of the ground.

Water

Water on the Earth flows downhill. Hydroelectric power plants use this movement to create electricity.

Solar energy

Light from the Sun provides solar energy. Solar panels can be installed almost anywhere, but only generate power during the daytime.

How can we use less energy?

Cycling

Cycling uses only human energy, so it saves the Earth's natural energy resources. It is cleaner for the environment and healthier for you!

Saving energy

Using less energy helps us stretch our energy sources further, and longer. Turning off the lights can help us to be good caretakers of our planet!

Nuclear energy

Huge amounts of energy come from splitting apart tiny particles. The radioactive materials used in nuclear plants must be stored safely.

Biofuel

Biofuels come from plants such as corn and sugar cane. These can be burned like fossil fuels in power plants or vehicles.

? Quick quiz

1. What is plant fuel called?

2. What kind of energy does the Sun provide?

3. Which type of power plant uses radioactive material?

See pages 132–133 for the answers

Answers

Page 9 1) The Sun came first. 2) Around 4.5 billion years ago. 3) The Earth is a rocky planet.

Page 11 Aurora.

Page 12 1) A meteor that has fallen to the Earth. 2) No. The Earth moves around the Sun.

Page 15 1) Yes. It is solid iron and nickel. 2) The aesthenosphere. 3) No. The crust is broken into segments, or plates.

Page 17 1) True. 2) True. 3) False. There is some gravity from bodies in space.

Page 19 Jupiter.

Page 21 1) 4 billion years old. 2) Yes. Crocodiles are related to dinosaurs. 3) 65 million years ago.

Page 23 A hippo.

Page 25 1) Over 3.5 km (2.17 miles) thick. 2) Around 10,000 BCE. 3) Yes. The location of New York City was under ice during the last ice age.

Page 28 1) False. It formed from lava produced by volcanoes. 2) True. 3) False. The Barberton Greenstone Belt, South Africa, is believed to be the oldest.

Page 31 1) True. 2) False. It becomes rock when it cools and hardens.

Page 33 1) Volcanic ash or mud. 2) Yellowstone National Park, USA. 3) 116 m (380 ft).

Page 34 1) False. Humus is the top layer. 2) True. 3) True.

Page 37 1) True. 2) True. 3) False. Minerals are not alive.

Page 39 1) b. 2) a.

Page 41 1) About 18,000 years ago. 2) Weathering. 3) Yes.

Page 43 1) Mineral deposits. 2) The Colorado River. 3) Sandstone.

Page 45 1) True. 2) False. They record movements of living things. 3) True.

Page 47 1) False. It is in Antarctica. 2) False. Some deserts are very cold at night.

Page 49 1) The surface of Thailand is made up of many caves and sinkholes.

Page 51 1) A stalagmite grows from the floor. 2) No. It is mildly acidic and only wears away rocks. 3) A column.

Page 53 1) Molten rock rises up through seafloor cracks and hardens. 2) Anatolia. 3) The Pacific Ocean plate.

Page 55 1) True. 2) True.

Page 57 1) Farmland. 2) Desert. 3) The Amazon Rainforest.

Page 59 1) False. It is a type of salamander. 2) False. A manatee is also known as a se cow. 3) False. They are differen species.

Page 61 1) A habitat. 2) A grove of Aspen trees in Utah, USA. 3) A tardigrade.

Page 65 1) True. 2) False. Cold water is carried from the North and South poles. 3) False. The are wind currents.

Page 66 1) True. 2) True. 3) Tru

Page 69 1) The mineral halite, or salt. 2) Seawater. 3) Yes. Seawater freezes at a lower temperature than freshwater.

Page 71 1) Around 4.5 billion years old. 2) Yes. The Earth wobbles over long periods of time – about every 26,000 year 3) The Sun.

Page 73 1) True. 2) True. 3) False. It is the Amaz River in South America.

Page 75 1) No. It is a lake. 2) No. Seas do. 3) The Sea of Marmara is the world's smallest.

Page 76 1) The Atlantic Ocean. 2) Angel Falls. 3) The Denmark Strait cataract.

Page 79 1) The Antarctic ice sheet. 2) Around 90 per cent. 3) A chunk of ice in the ocean that is smaller than an iceberg and a bergy bit.

Page 81 1) A long, winding ridge of sediment left by a glacier. 2) Yes. Glaciers move like rivers of ice. 3) The Lambert-Fisher Glacier in Antarctica.

Page 82 1) A mid-ocean ridge. 2) Challenger Deep. 3) Limestone.

Page 84 1) Light created by animals using chemicals. 2) The sunlit zone. 3) Yes. Giant squids exist.

Page 89 1) b. 2) c.

Page 90 1) Blue light. 2) Seven main colours blend to form millions of shades. 3) Yellow.

Page 92 1) 365 days. 2) No. Only some animals who live in places with very cold winters hibernate. 3) No. Different places are tilted towards or away from the Sun throughout the year. This means they have different seasons.

Page 95 Mount Kilimanjaro is a mountain with a mountain climate, which means it gets cold even though it is near the equator.

Page 97 1) Evaporation. 2) Water vapour is the gas version of water. 3) Meteorologists.

Page 99 1) Cirrus clouds. 2) Precipitation. 3) A cumulonimbus cloud.

Page 101 1) True. It only sometimes strikes the tallest spot. 2) True. 3) True.

Page 103 1) Table salt. 2) No. Cloud seeding uses clouds to try to make rain fall. 3) Water droplets.

Page 105 1) The Enhanced Fujita (EF) Scale. 2) A cumulonimbus cloud. 3) The eye of the storm.

Page 109 1) Around 10 billion. 2) Yes. The population is growing. 3) Tokyo.

Page 110 1) China. 2) The Pyrenees. 3) Great Britain.

Page 112 The woolly mammoth.

Page 115 Romulus and Remus.

Page 117 1) Wheat. 2) A combine harvester. 3) Animal husbandry.

Page 119 1) True. 2) False. North is the direction towards the top of the Earth. South is downwards. 3) False. It is shown by lines called contours.

Page 121 1) About 80,000 tonnes (88,185 tons). 2) Gyres.

Page 123 1) False. Only certain types of material can be recycled. 2) True. 3) True.

Page 125 1) c. 2) b.

Page 127 Venus.

Page 129 1) Oxygen. 2) Photosynthesis.

Page 131 1) Biofuel. 2) Solar energy. 3) A nuclear power plant.

Quiz your friends!

Who knows the most about the Earth? Test your friends and family with these tricky questions. See pages 136–137 for the answers.

Questions

1. What is the name of the **supercontinent** that existed around **330 million years** ago?

5. What is fossilized poo called?

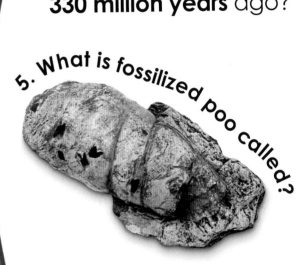

9. How much **warmer** was the Earth **56 million years** ago?

10. Which type of rock is made by lightning?

What is the **visible line** around the **middle** of the Earth called?

4. What is the **deepest** ocean zone?

3. How long would a day on the Earth be without the Moon?

8. Which place holds the **record** for the **hottest temperature** on the Earth?

6. What are **low, fluffy clouds** called?

7. Which term refers to large areas of **forestland** being **cut down**?

11. What is the name of the line where **space begins**?

12. What is the **largest desert** in the world?

13. What are **tiny bits** of broken-down **plastic** called?

14. What is the name of the landform that shoots out hot water?

15. How much of an iceberg is **underwater**?

Answers

1. Pangaea

8. The **hottest** temperatu
on record was at **Deat**
Valley, USA.

13. **Microplastics**

3. Without the Moon, a day on the Earth would only be five to six hours long!

4. Hadal is the deepest zone of the ocean.

2. The **Equator** divides the Earth into **two hemispheres.**

5. Coprolite

7. Deforestation

6. Cumulus clouds

9. The Earth was warmer by **7 °C** (12.6 °F) than it is today.

10. *Fulgurite*

11. The **Karman line**

12. Antarctica

14. Geysers shoot out hot water and steam.

15. **90 per cent** of an iceberg is underwater.

Glossary

acidic
Containing a chemical that can wear away certain materials

adaptation
When an animal develops features to help it survive in a certain area

air
Gases that form the Earth's atmosphere

artificial
Made by humans

ash
Small bits of rock that erupt out of volcanoes

atmosphere
Layer of gases around the Earth

atoms
Tiny particles that make up gases, liquids, and solids

axis
Invisible line through the centre of the Earth, around which the planet rotates

bacteria
Small living things that can usually only be seen with a microscope

bedrock
Layer of rock beneath the ground

biome
Area where animals and plants have adapted to survive in the climate

boreal forest
Cold biome with freezing temperatures for around half the year, also known as taiga

carbon dioxide
Gas found in the atmosphere that makes the Earth warmer

climate
Usual temperature and amount of precipitation in a specific area

cloud
Floating mass of water droplets or ice crystals

continent
Huge area of land, usually made up of different countries

core
Extremely hot centre of the Earth

crust
Outer rocky layer of the Earth

current
Flow of water, air, or electricity

desert
Area that receives very little precipitation, such as rain or snow

earthquake
Shaking of the Earth due to the activity of plates underground

ecosystem
Community of living things in an area

energy
Force that causes things to happen, such as movement

equator
Imaginary line running around the middle of the Earth

erosion
Movement of rock by wind, rain, or ice from one place to another

evaporation
Process of liquid water being heated to become a gas

extinction
When a species dies out completely

fossil
Remains of a plant or an animal or its activities preserved in stone

gemstone
Beautiful or valuable type of mineral

glacier
Large body of ice that slowly moves across land like a river

government
Group of people that run a country

gravity
Force that pulls things together

habitat
Area where a type of animal usually lives

Karman line
Imaginary line marking the place where the Earth's atmosphere ends and space begin

landform
Natural, rocky feature found on land or at the bottom of the ocean

a
olten rock that
s erupted above
e ground

htning
ectrical charge
at forms in clouds,
used by ice crystals
d water droplets
ashing into
ch other

agma
olten rock beneath
e ground

editerranean
ea around the
editerranean
a with typically
t summers and
ol winters

ineral
atural solids made
of crystal shapes

olten
mething that has
een melted into
liquid

oon
atural body that
bits the Earth

cean
rge body of water
at is not bordered
land

orbit
Path of an object
being pulled
around another
body by gravity

oxygen
Gas that animals and
fish breathe, found in
the atmosphere

petroleum
Natural liquid made
from the remains of
buried plants and
animals

planet
Huge, spherical
object found
naturally in space

plastic
Artificial material used
to make many items,
which does not break
down easily

plate
Large segment of rock
beneath the ground,
forming part of the
Earth's crust

polar
Icy area near to
the North or South
Pole that is cold all
year round

poles
Imaginary points at
the top and bottom
of the Earth

population
Number of people
in an area

precipitation
Water that falls from
clouds as liquid or ice

pressure
Force of something
pressing down on
another object

season
Period of similar
weather at a certain
time of the year

sediment
Small pieces of rock,
such as sand

solar
To do with the Sun

Solar System
The Sun and bodies
that orbit it

species
Type of animal or plant

star
Huge body of burning
gas in space

temperate
Mild climate zone
that usually has
warm summers
and cool winters

thunder
Sound made by air
expanding in clouds
because it has been
heated by lightning

tides
Movement of oceans
caused by the pull of
gravity from the Moon
and the Sun

tornado
Column of spinning
wind reaching from
storm clouds to
the ground

tropical
Warm climate zone
close to the equator

volcano
Crack in the Earth's
surface through which
molten rock erupts

weathering
When small pieces of
rock are broken off
larger rocks by wind,
rain, or water

Index

Acknowledgements

DORLING KINDERSLEY would like to thank: Caroline Hunt for proofreading, Helen Peters for the index, Abhijeet Dutta and Ishani Nandi for additional editorial help.

The publisher would like to thank the following for their kind permission to reproduce their photographs:

(Key: a-above; b-below/bottom; c-centre; f-far; l-left; r-right; t-top)

1 123RF.com: Wilfred Marissen (br); tebnad (fbl/Wind Turbine); Dr Ajay Kumar Singh (crb/Sunflowers). Dorling Kindersley: 01253854 (clb); Suhas Asnikar / Mangala Purushottam (clb/Bonsai, br/Bonsai); The Natural History Museum, London (crb/Butterflies). Dreamstime.com: Adambowers (cb); Cyberfyber (fbl, clb/Buildings, crb/Buildings); Igor Dymov (clb/Copenhagen); Sergey Uryadnikov / Surz01 (clb/Kelp Gull); Deymos (crb/Building); Tetiana Zbrodko / Ta (bl, crb/Chrysanthemum); Demerzel21 (br/Tower). NASA: NOAA / GSFC / Suomi NPP / VIIRS / Norman Kuring (bc/Earth). 2 Dorling Kindersley: The Natural History Museum, London (bl, bc). 3 123RF.com: Wilfred Marissen (crb/Spoonbill); tebnad (clb/Wind Turbine); Dr Ajay Kumar Singh (bc/Sunflowers, crb/Sunflowers). Alamy Stock Photo: Simon Belcher (br). Dorling Kindersley: 01253854 (cb/Frog); The Natural History Museum, London (cb/Butterflies); Suhas Asnikar / Mangala Purushottam (cb/Bonsai, crb); Twan Leenders (cb/Snake). Dreamstime.com: Adambowers (cb/Krakatoa); Sergey Uryadnikov / Surz01 (cb/Building); Deymos (cb/Building); Igor Dymov (cb/Copenhagen); Cyberfyber (cb/Buildings, cb/Buildings Left, clb/Buildings, bc/Buildings); Tetiana Zbrodko / Ta (clb/Chrysanthemum, crb/Chrysanthemum); Steve Byland / Stevebyland (bc); Ongchangwei (bc/Mountain); Demerzel21 (bc/Tower). NASA: NOAA / GSFC / Suomi NPP / VIIRS / Norman Kuring (bc/Earth). 4 Dorling Kindersley: Simon Mumford / NASA (cra). 5 123RF.com: Irina Pommer (tr). Alamy Stock Photo: World History Archive (c). Science Photo Library: Eye Of Science (bl). 6 123RF.com: Dr Ajay Kumar Singh (cra/Sunflowers); tebnad (tl/Wind Turbine, cla/Wind Turbine). Dorling Kindersley: Twan Leenders (cra/Snake); Suhas Asnikar / Mangala Purushottam (tl/Bonsai, tr/Bonsai). Dreamstime.com: Cyberfyber (tl/Buildings, cla/Buildings, cr/Buildings); Steve Byland / Stevebyland (fcl); Ongchangwei (cra/Mountain); Demerzel21 (cra/Tower); Tetiana Zbrodko / Ta (cla/Chrysanthemum, tr/Chrysanthemum); Steve Byland / Stevebyland (crb/Hummingbird). NASA: NOAA / GSFC / Suomi NPP / VIIRS / Norman Kuring (t/Earth). 6-7 123RF.com: Russ McElroy / russ9358 (b). 7 123RF.com: Wilfred Marissen (tl/Spoonbill). 8-9 ESA: NASA (Background). 10-11 Dreamstime.com: Serge Bogomyako / Sergebogomyako (c). 10 NASA: (bc). U.S. Air Force: (c). 11 123RF.com: filmfoto (cl); Russ McElroy / russ9358 (c). Dreamstime.com: Lars Christensen / C-foto (c); Ulkass (b/Clouds). 12 Dreamstime.com: Andras Csontos (cl). 12-13 Alamy Stock Photo: NASA / NOAA / SPL (c). 13 Getty Images: Barcroft (bl). 14-15 Dreamstime.com: Gardendreamer (tc). 16 Dreamstime.com: Andygaylor (cl). ESA: Herschel / PACS / MESS Key Programme Supernova Remnant Team; NASA, ESA and Allison Loll / Jeff Hester (Arizona State University) (bc). NASA: (bl). 16-17 123RF.com: swavo (Background). 17 Dreamstime.com: Dio5050 (cl); Alexander Pladdet / Pincarel (cb). Fotolia: robynmac (cb/Ball). 18 123RF.com: tebnad (cr). Dorling Kindersley: Suhas Asnikar / Mangala Purushottam (cra/Bonsai). Dreamstime.com: Cyberfyber (cra, crb); Tetiana Zbrodko / Ta (cbr/Chrysanthemum); Steve Byland / Stevebyland (crb/Hummingbird). NASA: JPL (crb/Venus). 18-19 NASA: NOAA / GSFC / Suomi NPP / VIIRS / Norman Kuring (c/Earth). 19 123RF.com: Wilfred Marissen (cr); Dr Ajay Kumar Singh (ca, cb/Sunflowers). Dorling Kindersley: Twan Leenders (cb/Snake); The Natural History Museum, London (tc); Suhas Asnikar / Mangala Purushottam (c/Bonsai). Dreamstime.com: Adambowers (tl/Krakatoa); Igor Dymov (fcla); Sergey Uryadnikov / Surz01 (tl/Kelp Gull); Deymos (tc/Building); Cyberfyber (ca/Buildings, cb/Buildings); Tetiana Zbrodko / Ta (ca/Chrysanthemum); Demerzel21 (c/Tower); Ongchangwei (cb). NASA AMES Research Centre: JPL-Caltech / T. Pyle (bc/Kepler). NASA: JPL / University of Arizona (ca). 21 Dorling Kindersley: The Natural History Museum, London (ca). Getty Images: Science Photo Library - Steve Gschmeissner (cra). 22 Dreamstime.com: Vhcreative (cla). 23 123RF.com: tritooth (br). Alamy Stock Photo: Universal Images Group North America LLC / De Agostini Picture Library (cra). Getty Images: Wild Horizon (cr). 24 123RF.com: jupiter8 (bc). Dreamstime.com: Songquan Deng / Rabbit75 (ca). 24-25 Dorling Kindersley: Simon Mumford / NASA (c). 25 123RF.com: Michal Bednarek (ca); Vadim Nefedov (tl). Alamy Stock Photo: Overflightstock Ltd (bc). Dorling Kindersley: Simon Mumford / NASA (cr). 26 Dreamstime.com: Anna Dudko. 26-27 Dreamstime.com: Bennymarty (c). 27 Getty Images: Ed Reschke. 28-29 Depositphotos: prudek. 29 Alamy Stock Photo: WaterFrame (br). 30-31 Getty Images: Handout / U.S. Geological Survey. 32-33 Dreamstime.com: Bennymarty. 32 Dreamstime.com: Lasenby (bl); Minyun Zhou / Minyun9260 (clb). 34 Dorling Kindersley: The Natural History Museum, London (crb). 35 Dreamstime.com: Pklimenko (ca). 36 Dorling Kindersley: The Natural History Museum, London (cb). Dreamstime.com: Kurhan (l). 36-37 123RF.com: donatas1205 (Table). 37 Dorling Kindersley: The Natural History Museum, London (crb). Dreamstime.com: Showface (b). 38 Alamy Stock Photo: Adam Eastland (cl). Dorling Kindersley: The Natural History Museum, London (tl). Dreamstime.com: Igor Kaliuzhny / Igorkali (crb). 38-39 Alamy Stock Photo: Marshall Ikonography (c). 39 Alamy Stock Photo: agefotostock Art Collection (cr). 40-41 Dreamstime.com: Baluzek. 41 Alamy Stock Photo: caia image / David Henderson (cla). Dreamstime.com: Lunamarina (cr). 42-43 Getty Images: Aaron Meyers. 43 Dreamstime.com: Josemaria Toscano / Diro (ca); Anna Dudko (cla). Getty Images: Arterra (cra). 45 Alamy Stock Photo: Stefan Sollfors (ca). Dorling Kindersley: The Natural History Museum, London (crb, cla). 46-47 Getty Images: Timothy Allen. 47 Alamy Stock Photo: Pavel Filatov (cr); Thomas Lehne (cra). 48-49 Getty Images: Marianna Massey / Stringer. 48 Getty Images: China News Service (br). 49 Alamy Stock Photo: Organica (clb). Getty Images: Pone Pluck (br). 50-51 Dreamstime.com: Mkos83 (b). 50 Alamy Stock Photo: imageBROKER / Michael Szönyi (bl); Andrey Nekrasov (clb). 52 Alamy Stock Photo: Newscom / BJ Warnick (ca). Getty Images: 1001nights (cl). 53 Alamy Stock Photo: Everett Collection Inc (tc); KEYSTONE Pictures USA (ca). 54-55 Dreamstime.com: Suwat Sirivutcharungchit. 55 Alamy Stock Photo: David Fleetham (ca). 56 Dreamstime.com: Alextara (crb/Savannah); David Steele (tr); Demerzel21 (crb); Jonmanjeot (bl). 56-57 Dreamstime.com: Christopher Wood / Chriswood44 (ca). 57 123RF.com: SHS PHOTOGRAPHY (clb). Dreamstime.com: Naturablichter (c); Seaphotoart (cr). 58 Dreamstime.com:

Alessandro Zappalorto (clb). Getty Images: Ed Reschke (bc). 58-59 Dreamstime.com: Littleny. 59 Getty Images: Joel Sartore, National Geographic Photo Ark (br); Reinhard Dirscherl / ullstein bild (cl). 60 123RF.com: Songdech Kothmongkol (bl). 60-61 iStockphoto.com: peeravit18 (c). 61 Alamy Stock Photo: Nature in Stock / Jan van Arkel (ca). Getty Images: "Diane Cook, Len Jenshel" (bl). Science Photo Library: Dr. Richard Kessel & Dr. Gene Shih, Visuals Unlimited (c); Eye Of Science (cb). 62 Alamy Stock Photo: mauritius images GmbH / Reinhard Eisele (t). Dreamstime.com: Tamara Kulikova (b). Dreamstime.com: Natursports. 64-65 Alamy Stock Photo: Bluegreen Pictures. 65 Dreamstime.com: Andrey Armyagov (cra). 66-67 Alamy Stock Photo: Grant Taylor. 66 Alamy Stock Photo: Jason Wells Nature Photography (fclb); National Geographic Creative / Josh Humbert (clb). Dreamstime.com: Tamara Kulikova (fbl). Getty Images: Kryssia Campos (bl). 69 Dorling Kindersley: Linda Pitkin (cra). Dreamstime.com: jeff waibel / Jfybel (cra); Natursports (cb). 70-71 Dreamstime.com: Oleksandr Kotenko. 70 123RF.com: Galyna Andrushko (clb); Łukasz Olszowiak (bl). Dreamstime.com: Eraxion (cb). 72-73 Alamy Stock Photo: Loetscher Chlaus. 72 Alamy Stock Photo: imageBROKER / Hans Blossey (clb); mauritius images GmbH / Reinhard Eisele (bl). 74-75 Dreamstime.com: Iuliia Kuzenkova. 74 NASA: Provided by the SeaWiFS Project, NASA / Goddard Space Flight Center, and ORBIMAGE (clb). NASA: Jeff Schmaltz, MODIS Rapid Response Team (cra). 77 Alamy Stock Photo: Alice Nerr (ca). iStockphoto.com: 13160449 (cra). 78-79 Getty Images: Jeff Vanuga. 78 Dreamstime.com: Achim Baqué (cra/Antarctica). Getty Images: Rick Price (cra/Ross). 80-81 Alamy Stock Photo: Colin Harris era-images. 80 Dreamstime.com: Peregrinext (cra). 81 Alamy Stock Photo: Tom Bean (cl); Ashley Cooper (cr). Dreamstime.com: Viktor Nikitin (cla/Ridge). 84 Alamy Stock Photo: Solvin Zankl / Lepidophanes Guentheri. Dreamstime.com: 111camellia (cb/Shark); Musat Christian (c); Harvey Stowe (bc). Getty Images: Joel Sartore / National Geographic (br). 85 123RF.com: Reto Kunz (cla/Noctiluca). Alamy Stock Photo: Nature Picture Library / David Shale (cra); NOAA (ca); Kelvin Aitken / VWPics (tc); Paulo Oliveira (cla/Mirrorbelly); Science History Images (bc). Dreamstime.com: Ppaula09 (tc/Jellyfish). FLPA: Norbert Wu / Minden Pictures (c, fcl/Black Swallower). Science Photo Library: British Antarctic Survey (cl/Sea-pig); Dante Fenolio (cra). 86 Getty Images: JC Patricio (bc). 86-87 Science Photo Library: Sputnik (t). 87 Alamy Stock Photo: Gary Dublanko (cra). 88-89 NASA. 89 Alamy Stock Photo: NASA Photo (cr). NASA: Tony Gray and Sandra Joseph (cra). 90-91 Alamy Stock Photo: Nawadoln Siributr (Used Thrice). 92 Alamy Stock Photo: Mihai Andritoiu (cra, br). 93 Alamy Stock Photo: All Canada Photos / Michelle Valberg (crb); Mihai Andritoiu (cla, clb). Dreamstime.com: Chuyu (ca). FLPA: Ingo Arndt / Minden Pictures (cb). 94 Dreamstime.com: Toniflap (ca). iStockphoto.com: narvikk (c). 95 Dreamstime.com: Steve Gould / Stevegould (bc). 96-97 Alamy Stock Photo: WILDLIFE GmbH. 96 Alamy Stock Photo: World History Archive (bl). 98 Dreamstime.com: Les Cunliffe (tr); Jin Peng (cr); Isselee (crb). 100-101 Alamy Stock Photo: Gary Dublanko. 102 Getty Images: JC Patricio (clb). 102-103 FLPA: Jim Brandenburg / Minden Pictures. 104-105 Getty Images: Cultura RM Exclusive / Jason Persoff Stormdoctor. 104 Alamy Stock Photo: US Air Force Photo (crb). Dreamstime.com: Sherah Martin (cra). 106 Dreamstime.com: Narathip Ruksa / Narathip12 (tl). 106-107 Depositphotos Inc: sunsinger (b). 107 Alamy Stock Photo: Simon Belcher. 108-109 iStockphoto.com: Starcevic. 110 123RF.com: jpchret (cla). Dreamstime.com: Alena Shchipkova (bl). 110 Depositphotos Inc: sunsinger (br). Dreamstime.com: Wilsilver77 (c). 111 Dreamstime.com: Janine Jeffery (c); Sufi70 (bc). 112 Alamy Stock Photo: Patrick Civello (c); Historic Images (bl); Jamie Pham (br). 113 Dreamstime.com: Narathip Ruksa / Narathip12 (cla/Rice Fields). iStockphoto.com: OGphoto (br). Library of Congress, Washington, D.C.: LC-USZ62-128561 (bl). 114-115 Alamy Stock Photo: Scott Wilson. 114 123RF.com: Irina Pommer (tr). 115 Alamy Stock Photo: Les Gibbon (cra). 116-117 Dreamstime.com: Stockr. 116 123RF.com: Carolyn Franks (clb). Dreamstime.com: Tropper2000 (bl). 117 Alamy Stock Photo: Avalon / Photoshot License (br); B Christopher (cr). 118 Alamy Stock Photo: Craig Leggat (c). iStockphoto.com: georgeclerk (c). 118-119 Dreamstime.com: Andrii Hrytsenko (c). 119 Alamy Stock Photo: Ian Rutherford (tl). 120-121 iStockphoto.com: luoman. 121 Alamy Stock Photo: Paulo Oliveira (cra). Dreamstime.com: Aquanaut4 (c). 123 Getty Images: J J D (br); jayk7 (cr). 124 Alamy Stock Photo: Daniel Dreifuss (cr). Getty Images: Chris Johns / National Geographic (cb). 124-125 Alamy Stock Photo: Tomasz Kowalski (bc); Genevieve Vallee (ca). 125 Alamy Stock Photo: inga spence (cl). Dreamstime.com: Eric Isselee / isselee (br); Piotr Marcinski (cr). 128-129 Dreamstime.com: Welcomia. 129 Dreamstime.com: Stockphototrends (br). 130 Alamy Stock Photo: Simon Belcher (cra). Dreamstime.com: Vanja Terzic (br). Getty Images: Maher Attar / Sygma (cr). 131 Alamy Stock Photo: Stuart Aylmer (bl); View Stock (cla). Dreamstime.com: Artranq (cra/Girl); Daniel Prudek (cl); Magomed Magomedagaev / Forsterforest (cra/Cycling). 132 123RF.com: tritooth (bc). Dorling Kindersley: The Natural History Museum, London (bl). 133 Dorling Kindersley: The Natural History Museum, London (br). 134 Dorling Kindersley: Courtesy of Dorset Dinosaur Museum (cr). 134-135 Dreamstime.com: Glasshoppah. 135 Dreamstime.com: Bennymarty (b); Scol22 (tc). iStockphoto.com: lucentius (cb). NASA: NOAA / GSFC / Suomi NPP / VIIRS / Norman Kuring (cr). 136 Alamy Stock Photo: Marshall Ikonography (l). 136-137 Dreamstime.com: Glasshoppah. 137 Dreamstime.com: Elena Duvernay (crb); Franz1212 (ca). Getty Images: by wildestanimal (bl). 140 Alamy Stock Photo: Stefan Sollfors (crb). U.S. Air Force: (br). 143 Dorling Kindersley: The Natural History Museum, London (bc). Dreamstime.com: David Steele (br)

Cover images: Front and Back: 123RF.com: Russ McElroy / russ9358 (Background); U.S. Air Force; Front: Dorling Kindersley: The Natural History Museum, London (cla); Dreamstime.com: 111camellia crb, Atorn Buaksantiah (Texture), Phanthit Malisuwan c/ (Texture), Tetiana Zbrodko / Ta cl; U.S. Air Force br; Back: Dorling Kindersley: The Natural History Museum, London ca; Dreamstime.com: Atorn Buaksantiah (Texture), Jan Kranendonk cra, Phanthit Malisuwan c/ (Texture); Science Photo Library: Eye Of Science crb; Spine: NASA: NASA Goddard ca

All other images © Dorling Kindersley
For further information see: www.dkimages.com